Grandma Elmaleh's
Moroccan
Cookbook

..Grandma Elmaleh in her dining room, proud of her sumptuous table...

GRANDMA ELMALEH'S
MOROCCAN
COOKBOOK

BY
LISA ELMALEH CRAIG

HESPERUS

Grandma Elmaleh's Advice to
All Who Read This Book:

'KHELLIHUM ITFAISHU'

which, translated from the Arabic, means:

'LET 'EM HAVE A GOOD TIME.'

Published by Hesperus Press Limited
28 Mortimer Street, London W1W 7RD
www.hesperuspress.com

First published by Hesperus Press Limited, 2012

Text and illustrations © Lisa Elmaleh Craig, 2012

The right of Lisa Elmaleh Craig to be identified as
the author of this work has been asserted by her in accordance
with the Copyright, Designs and Patents Act 1988.

Photography by Amani Hassan www.foodscapeblog.com

Designed and typeset by Madeline Meckiffe
Printed in Jordan by Jordan National Press

ISBN: 978-1-84391-363-4

TABLE OF CONTENTS

INTRODUCTION

Mme. Sarah Levy Elmaleh, my maternal grandmother, was a cook of extraordinary calibre. Craig Claiborne, the food writer of the *New York Times*, hailed her sumptuous table as being 'Moroccan cooking that a sultan would envy' (headline, *New York Times*, January 22, 1970). Her exotic repertoire was derived from several foreign cultures. She spent half of her eighty-odd years in Morocco in the seaport village of Essaouira, an ancient Portuguese fortress town on the Atlantic coast which eventually came under French rule. 'Mogador', as the French named it then, was indeed a melting pot of civilizations; Englishmen and Europeans, Berbers and Arabs of many tribes lived side by side with prosperous Sephardic Jewish merchants descended from Italy, Greece, Turkey, Portugal and Spain. Mme. Elmaleh's own ancestors were partially North African (probably Berber) dating back to biblical times, partially Sephardic Jewish from Spain, and partially Eastern European. Her father was a well-respected rabbi of somewhat mysterious origin; some say he was Eastern European and some say Palestinian, although no family member is absolutely sure.

As a young girl she was often shooed from the kitchen by her family's domineering Arab servants. Nevertheless, through persistent curiosity and an indelible memory, she retained much of their culinary techniques and was able to recreate and even improve upon this elaborate cuisine for her appreciative family and innumerable admirers since 1939, the year she and her husband, Raphael Elmaleh, brought their brood to America.

She was indeed a monument to the 'oral tradition', inasmuch as all of the recipes printed here had been passed on verbally from one generation to the next, and not one of her recipes had ever been written down until she and I worked together to create this book. I grew up at her side in the big white kitchen in Cedarhurst, New York. It was only a logical progression that led us to the many long hours of cooking, tasting, measuring and transcribing of her most prized recipes. (Ironically, Grandma herself had never used a single cookbook in her life.) Also, I decided to include many of her anecdotes and recollections which were a natural outflow from our long hours of cooking together.

Incidentally, despite the Arab and European origins of some

recipes, all of them adhere to strict kosher dietary laws; several of the recipes in this book are served only on Jewish holidays. Simply stated, kosher cooking means that no pork or shellfish may be eaten, nor may any meat products be cooked or served simultaneously with dairy products. Frying or sautéing meat in butter goes against the dietary laws, therefore vegetable oil (preferably peanut oil) is used instead. This is also beneficial to those readers who must watch their cholesterol levels and limit their intakes of saturated fats.

Fish, however, is not considered to be a meat (it is not nurtured from a mother's milk) and may therefore be served as part of a dairy meal, with bread and butter for example, and sour cream with fruit for dessert. It is considered 'neutral'.

It is easy to see why the Moroccan and Sephardic cuisines have blended so well together through the centuries, because Moslem dietary laws are very similar to those of Judaism. They eschew the use of alcohol whether used as a beverage or a cooking ingredient, and they are also forbidden the consumption of pork, ham, bacon or any of its by-products. The Arabs, however, may cook their meats with butter instead of oil, and readers may substitute equivalent amounts of

butter for oil if they so prefer.

Kosher salt or coarse salt is specified for all recipes in Mme. Elmaleh's repertoire. These salt crystals are far more flavorful than the iodized table variety. The Elmaleh women swear by it for all of their cooking, and they in turn have converted many other people to its virtues.

The reader may notice that the cooking times of the recipes are not always specific. Many of these recipes come from a time when days were unhurried and exact timing was of little importance. Cooking was a slow and sensual process; aromatic tagines were allowed to simmer and stew all day long. Nowadays, many of these longer-cooking dishes are readily adaptable to modern all-day 'crock' cookers.

Flexibility is a key factor here; the reader using this book must not be anxious about cooking foods exactly to the correct minute, because in most cases a little more or less won't hurt the overall result. The same goes for the quantities of ingredients. Please bear in mind that these recipes have been translated from measurements like 'handfuls' and 'glassfuls' into tablespoonfuls and cupfuls. The cook must keep tasting and testing, as there is no one absolutely correct way to prepare a dish. So relax and enjoy the sensory pleasure of 'cooking by feel'. The only rule of successful Moroccan cooking is that the end product must delight all the senses; it must please the eye, please the sense of smell and delight the palate.

Some of Mme. Elmaleh's recipes have already appeared in the *New York Times* (on two occasions) and in *Craig Claiborne's International Cookbook*, with many thanks to Mr Claiborne for bringing her talent to the attention of the public. She admired him greatly and considered him a very dear friend. Among those recipes already in print are her exemplary Moroccan Striped Bass with Cumin (see p73) and the tangy Orange and Olive Salad (see p49). Some of her more exotic dishes may call for such delicacies as orange flower water, pomegranate kernels, white truffles, cilantro (coriander) or saffron threads; fortunately nowadays most of these items are available at good specialty shops, if not directly in the 'ethnic' sections of local supermarkets.

I wish this book could provide the visual and olfactory pleasures of shopping in an outdoor 'souk' or marketplace in Morocco itself, with its tiled Moorish archways, *djellaba*-clad grocers, baskets of fresh spices, displays of shimmering brass pots and silver tea services, ornately decorated ceramic wares and abundant native fruits and vegetables. Imagine a glistening array of twelve sorts of olives... or fifteen varieties of dates.

Morocco is a rich and varied land with an exotic blend of cultures, and it is worth noting that, particularly in this time of strife in the Middle East, the enlightened Moroccan civilization was one in which Arabs and Jews lived side by side harmoniously for centuries, with the end result being not war and anguish, but love, mutual respect and a wealth of epicurean delights.

THE CULTURAL MIX THAT IS MOGADOR

It was a great temptation to title this book 'All-purpose Ethnic Cooking', because the cuisine of Mogador has been influenced by so many different worlds. It is fascinating to see how this charming microcosm-by-the-sea developed historically; the town's colorful history helps explain the diversity of the recipes in Grandma Elmaleh's repertoire.

In the seventh and eighth centuries, the Arabs moved westward from the Middle East with their Moslem religion and they invaded Morocco. Before that, however, the autochthonous people of Southern Morocco and the Atlas Mountain regions were the Berbers, and some of them had been converted to Christianity since the Crusades. Historians say that this strikingly handsome people, characterized by fair coloring and delicately chiseled facial features, are actually descended from the Vandals from East German Europe, who preceded the Romans to North Africa as far back as the fifth century. No one knows the exact origins of this strikingly handsome race; many have fair skin, blue eyes, even red hair. Their delicately chiseled facial features are more Caucasian than they are African, like their Mauritanian neighbors to the south. The Berbers had a culture and a language all their own, and many Moroccan romantics claim that they are actually descendants of the lost continent of Atlantis.

During the reign of the Ottoman Empire, there was a campaign to conquer all of the Arab countries in North Africa. Armies in the Moroccan realm, however, were able to fight off their invasion at Tlemcen, on the border of Algeria. For this reason, the Moroccan Arabic language never incorporated the Turkish tongue like all the other Arab-speaking nations. Two of the words they did adopt, however, were *calipha* and, of course, *pasha*, to denote important tribal chieftains. To this day, there is only about 40% language comprehension between Moroccans and their next-door neighbors in Algeria.

A writer for the Encyclopedia Britannica once poetically described Mogador, amid its 'sand dunes studded with broom', and its surrounding thickets of rare argan trees, as a city which 'bursts upon the view like a mirage between sky and sea'. Indeed, behind great fortress walls by the rocky surf, lies a shimmering diamond in the rough — a city of white-walled, sun-bleached houses, all trimmed with turquoise blue doors and shutters, with multi-leveled terraces and courtyards, and Moorish archways connecting ancient cobble-stoned streets. The narrow streets and alleyways are filled with people in *djellabas* and veils as well as in modern western dress. There are swarms of bicycles, donkeys and horse-drawn carriages. Mercifully, to this day, there are few automobiles.

Mogador appears as a prominent port on ancient European maps dating as far back as 1351. Even before that, however, there was a tiny island off its shore that still contains the ruins of a Phoenician factory which had been used to make purple dye from a certain species of sea creatures called murex. This purple dye was much prized because it was the color used in the making of robes worn by European royalty. The name Mogador has a rather odd source; it was supposedly named by Portuguese sailors after Sidi Megdoul — a holy man whose burial shrine had become a prominent landmark for their ships. In fact, this so-called saint had actually been named 'MacDougal', and it is presumed that this red-bearded Scotsman had been a Christian holy man or missionary in the land.

After the Spanish Inquisition, the Sultan of Morocco opened the ports of Mogador and Tangier to be a safe home for the Sephardic Jewish refugees. He guaranteed them protection as his special guests, and they were also exempt from military service. These refugees were to become some of the wealthiest trades-men on the continent of Africa, and their protected status continued to exist even under French rule.

The Portuguese, a culture of fishermen, took over the city in the sixteenth century and made it into a powerful citadel on the Atlantic. They built the 'Sqala', the massive ramparts, lookout towers, drawbridges and lines of cannon which still fortify the city against pounding waves and possible intruders. The Portuguese also contributed an indisputably great legacy of cuisine — their piquant vegetable salads and spicy fish dishes.

The recent town of Mogador was founded by Sultan Mohammed ben Abd'Allah in 1760 and its construction was completed in 1770. It has not changed much since. A grand entryway leads into the town through a monumental Moorish archway called the Bab Sebaa, or 'Lion's Gate', beyond which lie the labyrinthine streets of the town. The market square still looks like something from the Middle Ages; peddlers selling spices and aromatics, veiled women with fresh fruits and vegetables in their hand-woven baskets. Many craftsmen still sit in the doorways, cross-legged beside small stoves, hammering out the 'artisana' that is distinctive to Mogador — the arare wood furniture that is intricately carved and inlaid with designs in silver and mother-of-pearl. Mogador's housing was originally patterned after Roman architecture — white-walled facades built around sky-lit or open-air atriums. The interiors consisted of spacious high-ceilinged rooms with walls and floors decorated with bright blue-and-yellow Spanish or Portuguese tiles.

Mogador began its heyday as the busiest port in North Africa during the 1840s when the British came. They imported ostrich plumes from the Sudan and Central Africa, and spices, oils, barley and goatskins from Morocco. Along with silver tea sets, fine linen and clothing from Manchester, the British brought with them a new standard of elegant civilization. They established a strict school system. They heralded in a new era of decorum, refinement and etiquette that has remained a characteristic of native Essaouirans to this day. As a little girl, Grandma's highest praise was to be told that she behaved like 'a real English lady'. And those very proper English ladies shared with the natives their custom of social tea parties, introducing them to the art of baking cakes, biscuits and trifles.

While co-existence was essentially peaceful among Mogador's citizenry, there were still occasional threats from outside invaders. Early-twentieth-century townsfolk still recall a time when a barbaric tribal chieftain named Al Flous terrorized the city. He would impale the heads of his enemies on long spears at the Bab Sebaa, the entry gate of the city.

In 1912, Morocco became a protectorate of France. Grandma recalled vividly how, when the French took over, the culture of Mogador changed almost overnight. The British schools were closed down. Grandma's family, who had by now learned English with proper Oxford accents, in the words of those times, had to 'fold it up and put it away'. For the first time, she saw lipsticks and rouge being sold in the marketplace, and women who had previously eschewed make-up in order to be like British ladies, now were obliged to try it, to be like the French ladies.

Over the years, the French did much to modernize all of Morocco. They improved the public utilities and increased the level of education, establishing French as the official language, of course. In Mogador, they opened up the first tannery, and encouraged the export of 'Maroquinerie', the now-famous hand-tooled leather goods. The French also augmented the society-consciousness of Mogador's wealthy upper crust.

Grandma and Grandpa Elmaleh were by then married and living in a fairly affluent style. She accompanied him on many business trips to Europe and America, usually leaving their children at home with their devoted servants. She often returned with designer gowns from Paris, bed linens from Grenoble, silverware by Christofle, and children's clothes and popular music records from the United States. Life became more lavish, cosmopolitan and sophisticated. The French instituted a café in the main square of the town, they conducted Sunday tea dances at Mogador's first social club, and they popularized grand galas and formal balls.

Each mercantile family entertained shipping agents visiting from overseas — coming from England, France and Germany. For lack of fine restaurants, Mogadorians were obliged to regale them with sumptuous feasts in their own homes. And these visitors no doubt contributed their share of cultural and culinary ideas. Fine dining reflec-ted a family's warmth, refinement, and generosity, and such successful dinners launched many a

business deal. Thus, culinary artistry was elevated to an important status in the life of the city.

At the same time, however, Mogador was unknowingly losing its supremacy as a commercial seaport. In 1912, the French Marshal Lyautey began creating, from a small colony of mud huts, a more competitive economic stronghold so as to weaken the power of certain *ca'ids* and *pashas* who were still holding forth in Morocco's Southern regions. This modern, European-designed seaport to the north was called Casablanca. Over the years, major trade routes began to bypass Mogador in favor of this vast new port, and ultimately the little city sadly fell into a decline.

In 1939, Grandma followed her husband's business instincts and reluctantly packed up her family to sail to the United States. She knew very well that she was leaving behind a comfortable position in society — and what a society it was. A remote little jewel of civilization in which many foreign cultures lived together in harmony, protected by great stone walls against the sea. Fortunately, Grandma helped to preserve for all time Mogador's extraordinary culture — an exotic blend of native Berber and Arab dishes enhanced by Jewish, Portuguese, Spanish, English and French specialties.

As a postscript, it must be noted that today Essaouira is more international than ever; it has experienced a resurgence as a popular vacation

A BRIEF FAMILY HISTORY

destination for discerning jet-setters from all over the world. Many of its grand villas have been transformed into luxurious 'riyadhs' catering to tourists with an appetite for ocean breezes, swaying palms and exotic food.

Many years ago when Madame Elmaleh was growing up as little Sarah Levy in the small seaside town of Mogador, her own great-aunt, a much-respected woman in the community, boasted, 'I have the best, most virtuous daughters in all the land. Thank God they don't go to school and they don't dance.' Young Sarah's mother, Simchah, felt ashamed that she could not brag of the same qualities in her own

daughters. Quite the contrary; her husband, Rabbi Joseph Tobias Levy, was totally at odds with the old-fashioned Moroccan values. An enlightened and modern-thinking European man, he encouraged his daughters and sons alike to pursue the best educations available to them and to become accomplished in all the worldly social

graces. Indeed, he proudly accompanied Sarah to many dances himself.

Sarah grew into a lovely, intelligent and desirable young woman with dark brown eyes and long raven-black hair. At the age of sixteen she became aware of the attentions of the blond, blue-eyed young gentleman who lived next door. Her mother, fearing spinsterhood, felt that it was already high time for her daughter's betrothal, but Rabbi Levy, feeling that she was much too young, warded off her swain with admonitions that Sarah would eventually be 'marrying a nephew of his in America'. Nevertheless, the young man persisted; the nephew in America never materialized, tradition won out and in October 1916 Sarah Levy became engaged to Raphael Elmaleh at the ripe old age of eighteen.

After a customarily long engagement, the couple married in November 1917. The week before their first child, Victor, was born in November 1918, Sarah had a very prophetic dream. An aged rabbi with a long, white beard wearing a red and black turban appeared to her in her sleep and said, 'Tell Raphael to buy almonds.' She thought this rather peculiar, doubting very much whether Raphael had ever seen an almond. She rolled over to her other side to sleep again, when the same vision returned to her, this time more stern, with his two fingers pointed at her. 'This is the second time I tell you. Waken Raphael immediately and tell him to buy almonds.'

The next day, her husband followed her advice by cornering the market and buying all the almonds available in the marketplace. His success in exporting them at a great profit thus launched his brilliant career in the field of importing and exporting, which eventually earned him the affectionate title of Morocco's 'Almond King'. Unfortunately war was declared in September 1939. For safety's sake, he brought his family to America in November 1939. They rejoined Victor who had remained with his grandparents since 1926.

After the war, in 1946, Victor 'Americanized' his father's business to take advantage of the extra-territorial rights that American firms were entitled to.

The company imported a variety of things including sugar, tires, automobiles into Morocco until Moroccan independence in 1955, at which point the firm shifted its focus to the United States. As World-Wide Volkswagen, it became the first and last VW distributors, from 1954 to 1991.

In 1975, World-Wide went into the real estate business and is currently an important developer in New York.

Together, my grandparents made quite a study in contrasts. He was slight in stature and very fair, whereas she was tall, dark and very stately. His manner was quite elfin and whimsical, whereas her bearing was regal and proud. His tastes ran to seersuckers and comfortable shoes, while she much preferred brocade kaftans and tiers of ornate jewelry. Grandpa teased his wife mercilessly, constantly pricking her inflated sense of grandeur. He once asked to try some hair-growing formula that Grandma had. He came downstairs with one of Grandma's wigs on and said, 'Gee, this stuff really works.' She was not amused. His grandson, Tony, visited him toward the end of his life and asked how he was feeling. 'Not so good, God has forgotten me,' he said. Tony asked, 'Does God speak to you?' 'Yes,' he replied. 'What does he say to you?', Tony asked. 'I don't know. I can't hear him.'

Always full of mischief ourselves, my small cousins and I would most likely be hiding in the next room, convulsed with giggles. Furthermore, we entertained ourselves endlessly by mimicking their quarrels in our own 'Arabic' gibberish. But we worshipped them both, and they in turn spoiled us rotten. My own most vivid childhood memories are of Grandma's closet, a virtual Ali Baba's cave, glittering with brocade kaftans, ornate jewels cascading from gilded drawers and silver coffers, colorful silks, scarves, and myriad crystal perfume bottles — and maybe, just possibly, somewhere a trinket for me. To all of us grandchildren, she was a veritable Marco Polo. When they would return from one of their six-month voyages around the world, everyone would gather to help unpack maybe thirty-odd valises full of eye-popping treasures from the Occident and the Orient. And we children knew very well that we wouldn't be going home empty-handed. She was an exceedingly generous person. She was grand in everything she did and her largesse toward others — family, friends, as well as charities and organizations — was unsurpassed.

But back to the kitchen. After all, that was the pulsating heart of the household in Cedarhurst. Grandma invariably spent at least half of every day in there, in her long silk housecoat, with a tall glass of hot coffee in one hand, a cigarette (regrettably) dangling perilously out of the corner of her mouth, alternately arguing with the butcher over the phone and bantering in French, Arabic, English or Spanish with whomever 'the help' happened to be at the time. (The procession of servants — all of them characters — that Grandma hired over the years would fill another whole book.)

And the number of kitchen helpers always doubled around the holidays. In her proper Kosher household, Grandma had one large kitchen for non-dairy or 'meat' preparation, and another smaller kitchen for dairy dishes. That meant having two of everything — two sinks, two dishwashers, and two complete sets of kitchen equipment. Let us not forget the china. She had umpteen sets of each (a weakness, alas, which I have inherited), not to mention those fancy gilded sets which were reserved exclusively for festive occasions.

Very wisely, Grandpa refused to involve himself in Grandma's culinary domain.

Actually, this healthy distance was largely a function of self-preservation. After all the work Grandma and I did together, Grandpa's sole contribution to this cookbook endeavor was to impishly ask why, in all these pages, we neglected to include a recipe for soft-boiled eggs.

Grandpa Elmaleh eventually died just shy of his 103rd birthday, still dreaming of traveling on long ocean voyages. Grandma Elmaleh passed away in 1984 at the age of eighty-seven, after having lived a very rich and full life. Up until her passing, they continued to preside at the head of a very large banquet table in their grand old house in Cedarhurst, surrounded on holidays by at least twenty-five or more of their adoring family — brothers, sisters, nieces, nephews, children, grandchildren and later, great-grandchildren. And for so many wonderful and delicious years, we all felt very privileged indeed.

THE ORIGIN OF THE NAME 'ELMALEH'

The Elmalehs, my grandfather's family, are descended centuries ago from Spanish ancestors. In Spain their name had been 'Buenos hombres'. After the Inquisition, most Jewish families fled to other parts of the world. Those of the family who went to England translated their name to 'Goodman'. The French citizens called themselves 'Bonhomme', and the Israeli branch became 'Tovim'. Those of the family who traveled via Gibraltar into North Africa took the Arabic name 'Elmaleh'. Literally it means 'the good'.

BREAKFAST
DISHES

DEEP-FRIED EGGS À LA MOGADOR
(*Nzimat* – 'little stars')

We grandchildren referred to these as 'Cedarhurst eggs', because we grew up having them for breakfast on 'sleep-over' weekends at the huge Elmaleh home on Long Island. The eggs are crispy-crackly on the outside, smooth and creamy on the inside. These are guaranteed to make an 'egg-eater' out of any child.

2 eggs per person
3 tbsps oil
Fresh black pepper
Course Salt

1. Heat the oil in a large, non-stick pan.
2. Pour the eggs into the pan only two at one time. Either fry them until crisp and flip them and brown the other side, or very deftly (this takes more practice) keep turning the frying eggs in the oil as they crisp on all sides. This will give a rounder shape and a softer center.
3. When the eggs are completely crisped, lift them with a spatula and drain them slightly over the pan. Serve, sprinkled liberally with coarse salt and fresh black pepper. Begin frying the next batch, as needed.

SWEET CINNAMON COUSCOUS
(Sfaa)

This hearty cereal dish may just be the Moroccan equivalent of our oatmeal, or porridge. I have also eaten it in Moroccan homes as a light dairy lunch with salads, fruits, and mint tea on the side.

8oz (225 g) couscous
¼ cup oil
¼ cup water
¼ cup butter
Milk
Sugar
Cinnamon

1. Steam the couscous according to package directions, using the oil and the water as instructed.
2. When it has steamed fully, break the butter into little pieces and toss it through the couscous thoroughly so that it melts.
3. Steam it again for a few minutes.
4. Mound it high in a soup tureen or deep serving platter. Serve it in bowls with milk or cream, cinnamon and sugar on the side.

SONO TONO

During Passover, Jews are not permitted to eat leavened bread. Crisp, flat matzos are eaten instead, and at the end of the week-long holiday, it was and still is an Elmaleh tradition to prepare all leftover matzos in the following pudding-like dairy porridge.

1 box *matzos*
Coarse salt
Boiling water
1 stick butter
1 cup honey

1. Break the matzos up into smaller pieces and sprinkle them with coarse salt.
2. Place them in a large bowl and pour boiling water over them.
3. Let the matzos absorb all the water, then mash the matzos with a fork.
4. Tip the bowl carefully to drain off excess water.
5. While the matzos are still hot, cut a stick of butter into tiny pieces and toss the butter through the mixture until it melts.
6. Pour the honey over the mixture and stir it in. Serve this dish right away, while it is warm.

CINNAMON-HONEY BEIGNETS
(*Sfingi*)

These puffy, fragrant fritters make a festive breakfast, brunch or after-dinner treat. Make the batter the night before to allow it to rise sufficiently. They are very much like Italian 'zeppoli'.

MAKES 3 ½ DOZEN

1 cake yeast, dissolved in ½ cup hot (125°F) water
2–3 cups flour, approx
¼ tsp salt
Water
Oil for deep-frying
Honey
Cinnamon

1. In a large bowl, blend the yeast and water mixture, the flour and the salt. Stir it together to form a dough. Keep adding lukewarm water and stirring it until it spoons up loosely like a pancake batter.
2. Cover the batter with a damp towel and allow it to rise for 8 hours or overnight.
3. After the batter has risen for the allotted time, heat the oil for deep-frying in a wide pan. When it is hot enough, drop the batter by tablespoonfuls into the oil. Some dextrous Moroccan cooks actually form the batter into doughnut shapes, with holes in the middle.
4. Turn the *sfingi* to make sure they become golden on all sides. Remove them one by one to paper toweling to drain slightly.
5. Serve the beignets immediately on a large platter, drizzled all over with honey and then sprinkled with cinnamon to taste.

FLUFFY MATZO MEAL BEIGNETS
(Sfingi)

These are a variation of the previous recipe, except that Grandma prepared these during Passover. Because neither yeast nor flour is permitted during Passover week, this recipe uses only matzo meal and the beignets are 'leavened' by egg whites. Therefore, this dough need not be prepared in advance nor required to 'rise'.

MAKES 1 ½ DOZEN

1 cup matzo meal, soaked in 1 cup water,
  or enough to make a soft dough

4 eggs, separated

¼ tsp salt

Oil for deep frying

Honey

Cinnamon

1. In a large mixing bowl, beat the 4 egg yolks until light. Add the moistened matzo meal and blend well.
2. In a separate bowl, beat the egg whites with the salt until they hold stiff peaks.
3. Gently fold the egg whites into the matzo meal mixture. Make sure that this batter is homogeneously blended and fluffy.
4. Heat the oil in a wide skillet (pan or frying pan). When it is hot enough for deep-frying, drop the batter by teaspoonfuls into the hot oil. These beignets are slightly denser in consistency than the previous recipe, so these are made smaller in size.
5. Keep turning them so that they become golden on all sides. Then remove them to paper toweling to drain slightly.
6. Serve the *sfingi* immediately on a large platter. Drizzle them all over with honey to taste, then sprinkle them with cinnamon.

MOROCCAN ARAB BREAD
(L'khobz)

MAKES TWO 6" ROUND LOAVES.

1 package active dry yeast
1 tsp sugar
3 ½ cups unbleached flour
1 cup whole wheat flour or 1 cup rye flour
2 tsps coarse salt
½ cup lukewarm milk
Cornmeal
Aniseed and/or sesame seeds may be used if desired

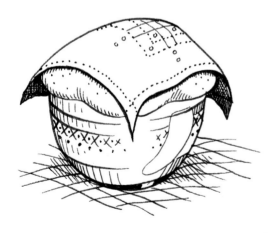

1. Dissolve the sugar in a ¼ cup of lukewarm water. Add the yeast and let it soften for 2 minutes, then stir and set it in a warm place to rise until the yeast is bubbly and it has doubled in volume.
2. Sift the flours together with the salt in a large mixing bowl. Stir in the lukewarm milk.
3. Add the yeast mixture into the flour milk mixture and add enough lukewarm water to form a stiff dough.
4. Put the dough on a lightly floured board and press hard with the fists, adding extra water if it needs to be made more elastic. Keep pushing the dough with outward strokes for about 10 to 15 minutes.
5. If desired, add the sesame seeds and/or the aniseed and knead well to distribute the seeds evenly throughout.
6. Divide the dough into two halves, forming balls of equal size. Let them rest on the board for 5 minutes.
7. Turn each ball out onto a baking sheet that has been lightly sprinkled with cornmeal. Additional aniseed or sesame seed may be as well, if desired.
8. Flatten each ball of dough slightly, forming a circle about 5 inches in diameter with a slightly raised center.

9. Let the ball of dough rise for about 2 hours in a warm place, covered by damp towels. Test the dough periodically with your finger; when you insert your finger into the dough, it should leave an indentation and not spring back into shape.

10. Preheat the oven to 400°F. Prick the loaves with a fork three or four times. Place them on the center rack of the oven for 12 minutes, then lower the heat to 300°F and bake it for 30 to 40 minutes more. When the bread is completely baked, it will sound hollow on the bottom when tapped.

11. Remove it and let it cool slightly. Slice each loaf into pie-shaped wedges and serve them warm preferably in a covered basket.

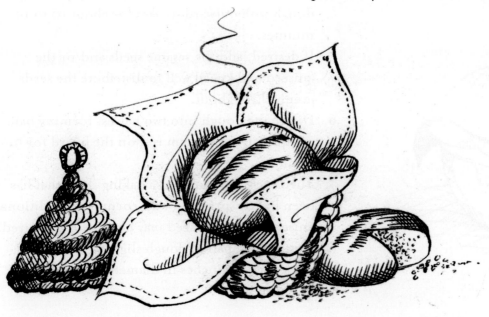

APPETIZERS

PASTELLITOS

Crisp and tangy, these little delicacies vanish quickly from the hors d'oeuvres platter. Each one is a miniature *pastella*, or meat pie, hence the name.

1 recipe for <u>*miga* meat filling</u> (see next recipe).

½ package of phyllo (or filo) pastry, thawed to room temperature

Deep oil for frying

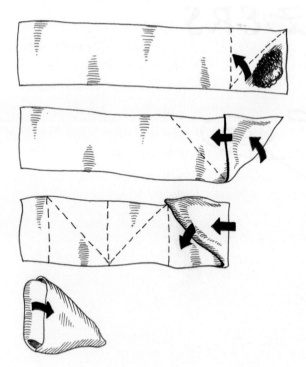

1. Place one double layer of the phyllo pastry on a board, and place a damp towel over the remaining sheets to keep them from drying and flaking.
2. With a sharp knife, slice the phyllo pastry into 3-inch strips, lengthwise.
3. Place one tablespoonful of the meat filling onto the lower corner of the first double-layered strip. Fold that corner up, in a triangle shape, to meet the side edge of the strip. Continue folding in this triangular fashion until the strip is almost used up. Tuck the remainder into a side 'pocket' of the triangle. Moisten the edges slightly and 'seal' like an envelope.
4. Continue this process until all the layers of phyllo and all of the *miga* are used up. Up to this point, the *pastellitos* can be made in advance, layered between sheets of waxed paper in a plastic container and frozen for later use. (Defrost them before deep-frying them.)
5. In a skillet (pan or electric frying pan), heat ½ inch of oil until very hot (350°F). Put several pastries in the pan in one layer, and deep-fry them first on one side, then on the other. When they become crisp and golden, drain them well on paper toweling and remove them to a serving platter. Serve *pastellitos* immediately — with napkins.

MIGA MEAT FILLING

This versatile meat filling is also the key ingredient for such main-dish casseroles as the noodle *pastilla*, the potato *pastilla*, and the deep-fried potato patties. The vinegar imparts an exotic tartness, and the mixture becomes velvety smooth. Grandma often doubled this recipe, freezing half of it. It always came in handy for unexpected guests.

1 ½ lbs (674 g) beef, ground round
2 large onions, peeled and coarsely chopped
One 8oz can Italian plum tomatoes, plus liquid
Coarse salt to taste
Fresh black pepper to taste
½ cup parsley, minced
2 tbsps vinegar

1. Place the meat, onions and the tomatoes into a large enameled pot with enough liquid to cover. Bring the mixture to a boil, and let simmer for a while, uncovered, until the liquid has nearly evaporated. Add salt and pepper to taste.
2. Continue cooking the mixture over medium heat, stirring occasionally to break up the lumps. Simmer the meat, uncovered, until the water has evaporated entirely and the meat is quite dry. This process may take a couple of hours. Do not allow it to burn.
3. Place the mixture into the meat grinder and grind it until it is fine and velvety soft.
4. Add the two tablespoonfuls of vinegar (or more, if desired) and the minced parsley.
5. Return the *miga* to the stove and cook down again, over low heat, until the vinegar evaporates. The mixture is now ready for preparation in the aforementioned recipes.

MIGA CHICKEN FILLING

Simply substitute 1 ½ lbs (674 g) cooked chicken meat for the ground beef in the previous recipe for *Miga* Meat Filling.

CIGARILLOS

These are crunchy 'little cigars' of liver and cumin seed, wrapped in crisp phyllo pastry.
They make excellent appetizers.

2 slices (1 lb, 450 g) beef liver
Coarse salt to taste
2 cloves garlic, minced
1 tbsp cumin seed, ground
1 tbsp oil
1 dash cayenne pepper (optional)
½ lb (225 g) phyllo (or filo) pastry, at room temperature
Deep oil for frying

1. Remove the skin from the liver slices and wash them. Pat them dry and salt them with coarse salt. Place them in the broiler (pan) and broil (grill) them for 5 minutes on either side. Be sure that they are cooked neither too rare nor too dry.

2. Place the liver in a meat grinder with the garlic, cumin seed, oil, and cayenne pepper, if desired. Grind it together twice to make a paste.

3. Fold each pastry leaf in half lengthwise, to make a strip about 3 ½ inches wide. Place a damp cloth over them to keep them from drying and flaking. Taking one sheet at a time, place 1½ tablespoonfuls of filling onto the edge of the strip, and roll it up tightly into a cigar shape. Seal the pastry by moistening the dough and firmly 'pasting' the ends closed.

4. Continue this process until all of the phyllo and the liver filling is used up. Up to this point, the cigarillos can be made in advance, layered between sheets of waxed paper, stored in a plastic container and frozen until later use. (Be sure to thaw them before deep frying.)

5. In a skillet (pan or frying pan), heat ½ inch of oil until very hot. Put several cigarillos in the pan in one layer, and deep-fry on all sides. They should be crisp and golden. Drain them slightly on paper towels and serve them immediately — again, with napkins.

CRUNCHY BEEF NUGGETS
(Khleh)

Turn leftover roast beef or pot roast into a bowlful of crackling good cocktail tidbits. *Khleh* is the Moroccan version of beef jerky. Coming from a land where refrigeration was scarce, this recipe is actually an age-old method of preserving meat. *Khleh* was originally prepared by nomadic tribes for their journeys on camel caravans. These are crunchy, juicy, and utterly addictive.

Leftover roast beef or pot roast, cut into 1" cubes
Coarse salt to taste
3 tbsps oil, approx.

1. Sprinkle the meat cubes with coarse salt.
2. Heat the oil in a wide skillet (pan or frying pan) until very hot. Add the meat and fry on all sides.
3. Turn the fire down very low and stir the meat occasionally, to make sure that it crisps on all sides. The *khleh* are done when a foam rises to the top of the meat and their consistency is hard and crunchy.
4. Drain them on paper towels and serve them immediately. They may be refrigerated or frozen and reheated at a later time.

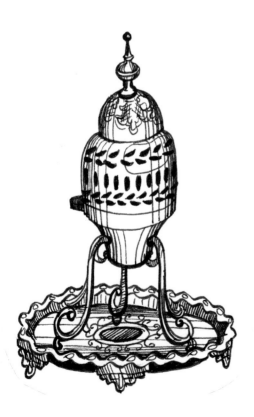

SOUPS

SWISS CHARD SOUP WITH CHICKPEAS

SERVES 6-8

1 large onion, peeled and chopped fine

1 beef shin bone, or any other beef bones
  with some meat intact

1 bunch Swiss chard, washed well, leaves and
  stalks shredded fine

Coarse salt to taste

Fresh black pepper to taste

Water to cover

½ cup fresh cilantro (coriander) or ½ cup fresh mint,
  minced (do not mix both)

2 cloves garlic, mashed

One 16oz (450 g) can chickpeas, drained

1. Put the first 6 ingredients into a pot and bring
   all to a boil. Simmer, covered, until the meat
   gets tender, for about 1 ½ hours.

2. 1 hour prior to serving time, make a paste of the
   cilantro, garlic, and salt and pepper to taste.

3. Blend this paste with ½ a cup of the soup.
   Return this mixture to the soup and blend well.
   Add the chickpeas and heat through. Serve.

PUMPKIN SOUP WITH CILANTRO (CORIANDER)

SERVES 8

½ large sweet (edible-variety) pumpkin, peeled, seeded and diced into 1" cubes

1 ½ – 2 large onions, peeled and sliced

1 beef shin, or any other beef bones with some meat intact

Coarse salt to taste

Fresh black pepper to taste

2 cloves garlic, mashed

1 tbsp sugar

Water to cover

One 16oz (450 g) can chickpeas, drained

½ cup fresh cilantro (coriander), minced

1. Place the first 8 ingredients into a large pot. Bring all to a boil and let simmer, covered, until the meat is tender, about 1½ hours.
2. Remove the bone, and add the chickpeas and simmer 30 minutes longer.
3. When fully cooked, purée the soup in a blender.
4. 30 minutes prior to serving time, stir in the half-cup of cilantro (coriander) and heat through. Serve.

cilantro (Kasbour)

EGGPLANT (AUBERGINE) SOUP WITH MINT

SERVES 6

1 large eggplant (aubergine), peeled and diced into
   1" cubes

2–3 onions, coarsely chopped

1 beef shin or flanken

2 tsps coarse salt

2–3 cloves garlic, minced

½ cup fresh mint leaves, chopped

Fresh mint sprigs to garnish

1 egg yolk

Juice of 1 lemon

1. In a large saucepan, bring the eggplant, onions, beef and coarse salt to a boil in water to cover. Let the soup simmer, covered, until the meat gets tender, for between 1–2 hours.

2. After the soup has cooked for 1 hour, add the garlic and the mint, and keep cooking until the meat is tender. Correct the seasoning.

3. Serve the soup in bowls garnished with a sprig of mint on top of each.

SEPHARDIC CHICKEN SOUP

This is not only a Jewish penicillin, but also an epicurean delight. Serve the boiled chicken pieces in a separate platter sprinkled liberally with coarse salt and fresh black pepper. Soul food.

SERVES 8

1 soup chicken, cut into serving pieces
1 beef bone, such as shin
½ cup parsley, minced
2 carrots, peeled and chopped
1 parsnip, peeled and chopped
2 stalks celery, with leaves, chopped
2 onions, peeled and chopped
Coarse salt to taste
Fresh black pepper to taste
½ cup cilantro (coriander), minced, optional
2 leeks, trimmed, well-washed and chopped
½ tsp turmeric or 1 tsp saffron water (see recipe)
Water to cover
1 cup soup
1 egg yolk
Juice of 1 lemon

1. Wash the chicken very well. Remove any sliminess from between the flesh and the skin, and rub the pieces all over with the rind of a lemon.
2. In a large saucepan bring the first 12 ingredients to a boil in water to cover.
3. Simmer the soup, covered, until the beef and the chicken are both tender, for about 1½ hours (note: if a young chicken is used in place of a soup chicken, the cooking time will be less). When done, remove the chicken to a serving platter.
4. Just before serving, if desired, blend on cup of the soup with the egg yolk and the lemon juice. Stir back into the soup and heat through. This will make the texture a little richer and add a tangy flavor.

MOROCCAN VEGETABLE POTAGE
(Harirah)

People of the Moslem religion fast all day during Ramadan, their month-long period of atonement, and they feast after nightfall on this rich and heartiest of soups. Served with fresh hot bread and a handful of dates, *harirah* makes a complete, nourishing meal. Grandma admitted to having learned this recipe from the Arabic household help back in Essaouira. It has lost nothing in the translation.

SERVES 8-10

½ cup barley

⅓ cup lentils

⅓ cup split peas

2 lbs beef shin, with bones, or equivalent amount of lamb shanks

3 tbsps vegetable oil

3 cups onion, chopped fine

3–4 stalks celery, including leaves, chopped fine

3 cups carrot, peeled and chopped fine

1 tbsp turmeric

10 cups beef broth and/or water

Coarse salt to taste

Fresh black pepper to taste

½ cup uncooked rice

1 cup canned, drained chickpeas

1 ½ tbsps flour

1 egg, lightly beaten

Lemon juice or vinegar to taste

¼ cup cilantro (coriander), chopped fine

1. Place barley in a bowl and add water to cover. Let soak overnight. If necessary, soak peas and lentils overnight too.

2. Cut the meat from the beef shin bones. Cube the meat into ½ inch cubes; reserve the bones.

3. In a large kettle (pot), heat the oil. Add the onion, celery and carrots and cook, stirring, until the vegetables become soft. Add the meat and continue to cook, stirring frequently, until the mixture browns. Sprinkle in the turmeric and add the bones. Stir in the beef broth or water and add salt and pepper to taste. Bring to a boil, and then simmer, stirring occasionally for 1 hour. Skim the surface once or twice to remove the foam and fat.

4. Drain and add the barley, peas and lentils and simmer for 15 minutes longer. Add the rice and chickpeas and simmer for 30 minutes longer.

5. Place the flour in a small mixing bowl and blend with a ladle full of soup. Return this to the kettle, stirring. Beat the egg with a ladle full of soup, and add it. Bring to a boil, but don't allow

it to boil. Add the lemon juice and cilantro and serve the soup hot. The soup will get thicker during refrigeration, so it may be necessary to thin it with broth or water when served again.

MINISTRA NOODLES

Ministra are dainty noodle squares that add interest to any plain soup, such as a chicken soup or a clear beef broth.

2 eggs, lightly beaten
Pinch of coarse salt
Flour, enough to make a dough ball 3" in diameter
Water, enough to make a dough ball 3" in diameter
1 egg yolk
Juice of 1 lemon

1. Knead the above ingredients together for 10 minutes, until the dough is smooth and elastic.
2. Roll the dough out onto a floured board. Roll it until it is very fine, about 1/16- inch thick.
3. Roll this sheet up loosely, jelly-roll (jam-roll) fashion. Allow the dough to stiffen and dry out for a few minutes.
4. With a very sharp knife, starting at one end of the roll, slice down into strips ¼-inch wide. Turn these strips and slice them crosswise into ¼-inch squares. Up to this point, these may be made in advance, dried, and stored in a dry place until later use.
5. Before adding to the soup, brown the noodles in a little oil in a separate pan. Add them to the soup and heat through until the noodles are tender.

SALADS

PIQUANT TOMATO SALAD
(*L'Merq Hazina* – 'The Mourner's Soup')

Glistening like a bowl of jewels, this zesty salad greatly complements any roast meat. Guests may fan their tongues, but they'll go back for seconds and thirds. This dish is particularly flavorful when garden-fresh tomatoes are in season, in late summer. For those who prefer a milder flavor, the hot peppers may be omitted; the salad will be equally delicious.

SERVES 8

4 fresh tomatoes, cored and minced

Juice of ½ lemon

½ preserved lemon (see recipe), minced

1 celery heart, minced, or 2 outer stalks, minced

½ cup parsley, minced

2 hot peppers (red pepperoncini), minced, or to taste

3 tbsps capers, with 1 tsp liquid

2 green peppers, minced

¼ cup olive oil

Coarse salt to taste

Fresh black pepper to taste

½ tsp cayenne pepper or less, to taste

1 clove garlic, minced

1. Mix all of the above ingredients together and let the salad marinate for 2 hours in the refrigerator. This salad is best served at room temperature for maximum flavor.

Incidentally, after a day or so, the leftovers will release a juice (hence the term 'soup') that makes delightful dunking with fresh bread. It is rather similar to Spanish gazpacho.

BROILED (GRILLED) PEPPER SALAD

SERVES 6

6 green, red and/or yellow peppers (a colorful
   mixture is best)

Juice of 1 lemon, plus extra juice to sprinkle on top
   before serving

2 tbsps capers, with 1 tbsp liquid

1 tsp coarse salt, or to taste

Fresh black pepper to taste

2 tbsps olive oil or argan oil*

1 garlic clove, minced (or more, to taste)

1. Cut the peppers in half and remove the seeds and
   stems. Place the peppers on a baking sheet, skin
   side up, in a 500°F oven for about 15 minutes or
   until the skin chars and separates from the
   peppers' flesh. Remove the peppers and allow
   them to cool.

2. When cool enough to handle, peel the peppers
   and slice them into strips about 3-inch by
   ½ inch.

3. Salt the strips liberally, while placing them in a
   mixing bowl.

4. Add the remaining ingredients and toss well.
   Correct the seasoning.

5. Arrange the strips in an elongated fashion in a
   serving dish. Refrigerate until serving time.

6. Sprinkle liberally with additional fresh lemon
   juice just prior to serving.

* Argan oil comes from a tree which is indigenous to Southwestern Morocco, in the region of
Essaouira. It has a rather acrid taste which takes some getting used to, but Grandma especially
liked it in the above salad. It is difficult to find in the West, if at all, and olive oil is certainly
just as good.

TOMATO SALAD WITH BASIL AND SCALLIONS (SPRING ONIONS)

Sweet, red tomatoes picked ripe from the garden make this salad especially delicious. Its freshness enhances the 'outdoors' flavor of barbecued meats, such as grilled lamb or _Kefta_ (see recipe).

SERVES 6

4 large ripe tomatoes, sliced ¼" thick
1 clove garlic, sliced
4–5 scallions (spring onions), chopped fine
2/3 cup fresh basil leaves, minced
Vinaigrette sauce (see recipe)

1. Arrange tomato slices in an overlapping, circular pattern on a flat serving platter.
2. Rub the tomato slices all over with the slices of garlic. Either add the garlic slices or discard them, according to your taste.
3. Sprinkle with the scallions all over, and then sprinkle with the basil.
4. At serving time, pour the vinaigrette sauce over all.

* * * * * * * *

FENNEL SALAD

Fennel, with its zesty anise flavor, clears the palate nicely between courses.

1 fennel bulb, trimmed of tough outer stalks
Vinaigrette sauce (see recipe)

1. Slice the fennel bulb lengthwise into 1/8- inch strips.
2. Arrange in a serving dish and drizzle the vinaigrette sauce over all.

··fennel··

ENDIVE (CHICORY) AND WALNUT SALAD

SERVES 6

4 large heads of Belgian endive (chicory)
½ cup walnut meats chopped coarsely
Vinaigrette sauce (see recipe), with 1 tsp
   sugar added.

1. Trim the endives of any withered outer leaves.
   Slice off the discolored base of each.
2. Quarter the endives lengthwise. Chop these strips
   in half. Place the endive in a serving dish.
   Sprinkle with the chopped nuts.
3. Pour the vinaigrette sauce over all.

* * * * * * * * *

BEET AND ONION SALAD

SERVES 6

One 8oz (225 g) can of sliced beets, rinsed and drained
1 large onion, sliced into 1/8-inch rings
½ cup parsley, minced
1 tbsp oil
2 tbsps vinegar
½ tsp sugar
1 tsp coarse salt
Fresh black pepper to taste

1. Place beets and onions in a bowl.
2. In a smaller bowl, blend together the remaining
   ingredients.
3. Pour the dressing over all, toss well, and allow the
   salad to marinate for 1 hour or so before serving.

SWISS CHARD SALAD
(Sulq)

SERVES 6

1 bunch Swiss chard, well-washed, cut into
   4" pieces (leaves intact)

1 cup water

1 clove garlic, minced

1 tsp cumin seed, ground

2 tbsps oil

Coarse salt to taste

1 tbsp lemon juice

1. Place all ingredients in a saucepan and bring to a boil. Simmer uncovered, until all the water has evaporated.
2. Serve warm if desired, or chill for several hours and serve as a salad. Sprinkle with fresh lemon juice just prior to serving, if desired.

COOKED CARROT SALAD WITH CUMIN

SERVES 8

1 bunch carrots, peeled and trimmed
1 tbsp oil
1 tsp coarse salt
1 clove garlic, peeled and minced
Water to cover
1 tbsp olive oil
½ cup parsley, minced
Juice of ¼ lemon
½ tsp cumin seed or more, to taste
½ tsp paprika
Dash of cayenne pepper (optional)
Coarse salt to taste

1. Place first 5 ingredients in a saucepan and bring to a boil, covered, until the carrots are tender but still firm.
2. Remove the carrots from the liquid and slice them into coins either with a knife or a ruffle-edged fruit cutter.
3. Toss the carrots together in a bowl with the remaining ingredients. Allow to marinate in the refrigerator for 1 hour or so before serving time. Correct seasoning if necessary.

* * * * * * * * *

CARROT SALAD WITH RAISINS AND NUTS

SERVES 4–6

3–4 large carrots, peeled and grated
½ cup walnut meats, coarsely chopped
½ cup golden and/or dark raisins
Juice of ½ lemon
Coarse salt to taste
2 tsps honey
Dash of cinnamon, if desired
2 tbsps mayonnaise or more, as needed, to bind

1. Blend all ingredients together in a mixing bowl.
2. Transfer to a salad bowl and serve.

COOKED SALAD

This tasty salad can also be spread onto a pizza crust and baked into a piquant 'Moroccan-style' pizza. Just sprinkle it with mozzarella and parmesan and broil (grill).

SERVES 4-6

6–8 fresh plum tomatoes or one 16oz (450 g) can Italian plum tomatoes, drained

3 green peppers, seeded and sliced into ¼" strips

1 hot chilli pepper, seeded and sliced into ¼" strips

2 tbsps oil

3 cloves garlic, minced

Coarse salt to taste

1. If using fresh tomatoes, pour boiling water over them for a few minutes and then peel the skins off.
2. Place all ingredients in a pot and cook slowly over a low fire until it is thick, like the consistency of jam.
3. Serve it cold as a salad. Stored in a sterilized jar, this compote can keep for a long time.

ORANGE AND OLIVE SALAD

This rather exotic combination of ingredients is surprisingly successful with native Americans as well as North Africans. Clementines, peeled and sectioned, may be used for part of the oranges — this makes a delightful variation. Any leftover salad releases a 'gravy' the next day that makes for superb dunking with fresh bread.

SERVES 6

5 sweet navel oranges, peeled and diced (Note: if the oranges are very tart, they may be sweetened with sugar before adding them to the salad)

¾ cup black salt-cured (shriveled) olives, halved and pitted

2–3 cloves garlic, minced

1 tsp coarse salt, or to taste (depending on the saltiness of the olives)

1 tsp paprika

½ cup parsley, minced

½ tsp ground cumin (optional)

1 dash of ground cayenne pepper (or to taste)

1 tbsp olive oil

1. Place olives and oranges in a bowl.
2. In a smaller bowl, mix together the remaining ingredients. Pour this dressing into the orange and olive mixture and toss all together well.

ORANGE SALAD WITH POMEGRANATES

Orange blossom water imparts an intoxicating fragrance to these fruit salads. Rose water may be used instead, and both extracts may be found in gourmet shops.

SERVES 6

3 navel oranges, peeled and chopped
3 pomegranates, peeled, seeds removed from pulp
1 tsp sugar
1 tbsp orange flower water
Dash of cinnamon, if desired

1. Toss the first 3 ingredients together and allow them to macerate for 1 hour or so in the refrigerator.
2. Before serving, sprinkle the salad all over with the orange water to 'perfume' it.

* * * * * * * * *

POMEGRANATE AND WALNUT SALAD

This salad always reminded me of a bowlful of glistening rubies. It has a very heady aroma and a crunchy-juicy texture.

SERVES 4–6

3 pomegranates, peeled, seeds separated from skin
1–2 tbsps sugar, or to taste
Dash of cinnamon, or to taste
1 cup walnut meats, coarsely chopped
1 tbsp orange flower water or rose water

1. Toss the pomegranate seeds, sugar and cinnamon together and allow the mixture to macerate in the refrigerator for 1 hour or so.
2. Before serving, stir in the walnuts and splash with the orange or rose water.

ORANGE AND WALNUT SALAD

SERVES 6

4 navel oranges, peeled and sliced into ¼" thick
  circles

1–2 tsps sugar, or to taste

2 tbsps orange flower water

½ cup walnut meats, coarsely chopped

Dash of cinnamon

1. Arrange the oranges decoratively on a serving
   platter.
2. Sprinkle with the sugar, then the orange flower
   water.
3. Sprinkle all over with the walnuts, and then
   sprinkle the cinnamon all over to decorate.
   Serve immediately.

HAROSET

Haroset is served during the Seder meal each year at Passover. It is a symbolic food which represents the clay and mortar that the Jewish people used in making bricks for the Egyptian pharaoh who enslaved them. Each family has its own special recipe; herewith Mme. Elmaleh's version. It is customarily served as a spread on lettuce leaves or matzos.

MAKES 1 ½ – 2 CUPS

2 apples, peeled and chopped
4–5 dates, pitted and chopped
½ cup walnut meats, chopped
4–5 dried figs, chopped
½ cup raisins
¼ tsp cinnamon, or to taste
1 tbsp sugar
½ cup sweet red wine (usually the sacramental
for the Seder)

1. Blend all the ingredients together, except the wine.
2. Pass the mixture through the grinder.
3. Stir in the wine and blend well.

VEGETARIAN DISHES

SWISS CHARD WITH LEMON AND GARLIC

SERVES 4-6

1 bunch Swiss chard, stalks separated and well-washed

1 tsp coarse salt

1 clove garlic, peeled and sliced

2 tbsps chicken fat or oil

Juice of ½ lemon

Coarse salt to taste

Fresh black pepper to taste

1. Bring a large kettle of water to a rolling boil with the teaspoonful of salt. Add the Swiss chard and let the water boil for 3 or so minutes, just enough so that the leaves become tender and brilliant green. Do not overcook.
2. Drain and rinse the chard under cold water to stop the cooking and seize the juices.
3. In a skillet (pan or frying pan), heat the chicken fat or oil. Add the garlic and sauté until tender, but do not brown it.
4. Add the chard, salt, and pepper and sauté lightly, until heated through and the flavors are blended.
5. Toss the chard with the lemon juice, and serve it in a dish garnished with extra lemon wedges, if desired.

swiss chard

STRING BEANS WITH TOMATO AND GARLIC

SERVES 4-6

1 lb (450 g) string beans, washed and trimmed
One 16oz (450g) can tomato juice
½ cup beef or chicken gravy, if available
1 clove garlic, peeled and minced
Coarse salt to taste
Fresh black pepper to taste

1. Place beans in a saucepan and add enough tomato juice to cover (reserve the rest for another use). Add the gravy, garlic, salt and pepper.
2. Bring all to a boil and simmer, partially covered, for about 10–20 minutes, (depending on the quality of the beans), or until the beans are tender and the sauce is somewhat reduced.

❋ ❋ ❋ ❋ ❋ ❋ ❋ ❋

FENNEL WITH SAFFRON
(*Fenuki* – from the Italian 'Finocchio')

SERVES 8

4 fennel bulbs, trimmed of any tough outer stalks
¼ tsp saffron leaves or 1 tsp <u>saffron water</u> (see recipe)
1 tbsp lemon juice
1 tbsp oil
1 ½ cups chicken broth or water

1. Quarter the fennel bulbs lengthwise. Trim off any excess or withered leaves.
2. Place all ingredients in a shallow saucepan, with enough liquid to cover.
3. Bring all to a boil and then simmer, partially covered, for about 20 minutes, or until the fennel is tender and the sauce is somewhat reduced.

EGGPLANT (AUBERGINE) AND CUMIN PURÉE
(El Berranniah)

SERVES 6-8

1 whole eggplant (aubergine), washed

3 cloves garlic, slivered

1 tsp paprika

1 tsp ground cumin

1 tbsp vinegar

1 tbsp olive oil

1/8 tsp ground cayenne pepper (optional)

1. Preheat the oven to 350°F.
2. Pierce the eggplant about twenty times with a sharp pointed knife.
3. Insert a sliver of garlic into each hole. Bake the eggplant in a 350°F oven for 2 hours.
4. When the eggplant is very tender, remove it and allow it to cool until it can be handled.
5. Scoop out all the pulp and place it in a bowl. Add the remaining ingredients and mash all together with a fork to make a paste. This dish can be served warm or cold. It is an excellent appetizer when spread on warm pita bread or crackers.

DEEP-FRIED EGGPLANT (AUBERGINE) WITH GRANDMA'S CHARISSA SAUCE

SERVES 4-5

1 large eggplant (aubergine)
Coarse salt
1–2 eggs, lightly beaten
1 cup matzo meal or breadcrumbs, for dredging
Oil for deep frying
Grandma's *Charissa* sauce (see recipe)

1. Slice the stem off the eggplant and peel the vegetable in alternate 'rows' so as to form lengthwise stripes.
2. Slice the eggplant into rounds ¼-inch thick. In a colander make a layer of the slices and salt them liberally. Keep layering and salting all of the slices. Set the colander aside to allow the eggplant to 'sweat' off its juices. This will take about 30 minutes.
3. When the eggplant has drained a bit, dry the slices off thoroughly in paper toweling.
4. Heat the oil for deep frying in a wide skillet (pan or frying pan).
5. Dip the eggplant slices first in the beaten egg, then in the matzo meal or breadcrumbs. Coat them well.
6. Deep-fry the slices until golden on both sides. Remove them to paper toweling to drain off excess oil. These can be served at this point, with *charissa* sauce on the side, or they may be layered in a baking dish to be reheated in the oven at a later time.

HONEYED EGGPLANT (AUBERGINE) PURÉE
(Zalooq)

'Branniah' is a relish or side dish which is customarily served in the Elmaleh home at Rosh Hashanah, the Jewish New Year. It was always the one item in grandma's culinary repertoire that, as a child, I stubbornly refused to taste. Older now and more adventurous, if not wiser, I too have come to appreciate this rather odd concoction.

1 large eggplant (aubergine)
2–3 tbsps oil
3–4 tbsps honey
1 tsp cinnamon
1 tbsp toasted sesame seeds

1. Peel the eggplant in alternate rows, to make a striped pattern. Slice the eggplant into ¼-inch slices.
2. Heat the oil in a wide skillet (pan or frying pan), and brown the eggplant slices very well on both sides, until they are dark brown – almost black.
3. Drain the slices and pat them dry in paper toweling.
4. In a medium saucepan, cook the slices together with the honey, cinnamon and sesame seeds. Stir constantly with a wooden spoon until all the eggplant is mashed, the honey is absorbed, and all is blended to a smooth consistency.
5. Store the purée in an airtight jar. It will keep in the freezer and in the refrigerator for a long time.

CANDIED EGGPLANTS (AUBERGINES) WITH GINGER
(Ptljan)

These make a sweet and pungent relish to serve with meat.

10 tiny eggplants (aubergines), washed, with stems intact.

1 tsp coarse salt

Water to cover

1½ cups sugar or honey, or half of each

1 tbsp powdered ginger

1. Pierce the eggplants all over with the tines of a fork.
2. Bring them to a boil in salted water to cover. Let them cook for 30 minutes or until they are tender. Drain.
3. Squeeze the eggplants in paper toweling until they are dry.
4. In a wide, heavy saucepan, add the sugar with enough water just to cover it.
5. Add the eggplants and let them simmer over a slow fire, turning them constantly so that they become well coated and they absorb the sugar. Cook them this way until the sugar is almost completely absorbed into the eggplant.
6. Add the powdered ginger and stir well. Put the eggplants in airtight jars and store them at room temperature in a cool, dry place. After opening a jar, store the remainder in the refrigerator.

ARTICHOKES À LA MAROCAINE
(El Qoq)

SERVES 6

6 artichokes, trimmed of stalks and any discolored outer leaves (Rub all the cut edges with fresh lemon juice to keep the artichokes from turning black.)

½ lemon, sliced thin

2 cloves garlic, peeled and slivered

1 tsp coarse salt

1 tbsp oil or chicken fat

Vinaigrette sauce, optional (see recipe)

1. In a large saucepan (do not use aluminum because it affects the taste of the vegetable and the pot may blacken) place the artichokes, lemon, garlic, salt and oil. Add water to cover.

2. Bring to a boil and allow to boil, covered, over low heat for 30 to 40 minutes, or until the outer leaves can be picked off easily.

3. Serve the artichokes warm or refrigerate them and serve them cool. To eat, tear each artichoke leaf off individually and dip the 'fleshy' end into the vinaigrette sauce, discarding the tougher parts of the leaf.

ARTICHOKE BOTTOMS WITH TURMERIC

SERVES 6

6 artichokes, stalks intact
½ lemon, sliced thin
½ lemon, peeled and chopped fine
½ tsp turmeric
1 tbsp coarse salt
1 qt water
1 tbsp oil or chicken fat
2 cloves garlic, crushed

1. Trim away all leaves from the artichokes, leaving the stalks intact. With a sharp pointed knife cut around the fuzzy choke part and remove it. Halve or quarter the artichokes lengthwise. As this is done, put the artichokes immediately into a bowl with the lemon slices and water to cover.

2. Bring the pot of water to a boil with the chopped lemon, the turmeric, the salt, the shortening and the garlic.

3. When the water has boiled, put in the artichoke pieces.

4. Simmer them slowly, until the water has evaporated and only the oil remains as a sauce.

CARDONES (CARDOONS) WITH LEMON AND TURMERIC
(Kharchouf)

Cardones (sometimes called cardoons) are long-stalked celery-like vegetables, which are related to the thistle family. They can be obtained from Italian greengrocers. When cooked, they are tender and translucent, with a flavor reminiscent of artichokes.

SERVES 8

1 bunch cardones, peeled and trimmed of stringy fibers on stalks

1 lemon, peeled, seeded and chopped

½ tsp turmeric

1 tbsp coarse salt

2 tbsps oil or chicken fat

2 cloves garlic, peeled and crushed

Water or chicken broth to cover

1. Cut the cardone stalks into 6-inch stalks and immerse immediately in a bowl of water with I tablespoonful of lemon juice to keep them from discoloring.

2. Place the prepared cardones in a pot with the remaining ingredients.

3. Bring all to a boil. Cover the pot partially and simmer the vegetables until they are very tender and the liquid has reduced quite a bit. Do not let them burn; because of the lemon, the cardones should remain light-colored.

• Kharchouf •

STUFFED PEPPERS, VEGETARIAN STYLE

SERVES 6-8

Vegetable stuffing:

1 carrot, chopped fine

½ cup parsley, minced

2 stalks celery, minced

1 onion, chopped fine and fried golden brown

1 raw onion

½ cup raw mushrooms, chopped

1 hard-boiled egg, minced

1 cup matzo meal or cracker meal

Coarse salt to taste

Fresh black pepper to taste

½ tsp cinnamon

½ tsp nutmeg

8 long frying peppers, cored and seeded, left whole
  or 4 large sweet peppers, halved lengthwise, cored
  and seeded

½ cup oil

1 cup tomato juice

1 cup water

1. Preheat the oven to 350°F.

2. Blend together all of the stuffing ingredients. Let stand a few minutes so that the matzo meal fluffs up. Pass through a grinder.

3. Stuff the long frying peppers whole, or else stuff the sweet pepper halves. In a wide skillet (pan or frying pan) heat the ½ a cup of oil and fry the peppers (skin side down) to loosen their skin. Peel off as much of their skin as possible.

4. Place the stuffed peppers in a baking dish and pour the remainder of the frying oil all over them.

5. Add the tomato juice and the water to the baking dish and bake the peppers for 1 hour at 350°F.

BEAN CASSEROLE WITH CILANTRO (CORIANDER)
(Loubia)

The following can be a side dish or it can be converted into a meat course simply by adding as much lamb stew meat as desired.

SERVES 8-10

1–2 lamb shanks, whole, or 1 lamb breast (or more if desired), cubed

1 pkg navy beans, soaked overnight in water to cover

1 large onion, chopped

1 tbsp oil

2–3 cloves garlic, minced

One 8oz (225g) can Italian plum tomatoes, with liquid

1 cup fresh cilantro (coriander), chopped, plus ½ cup for garnish

1 tsp turmeric

Coarse salt to taste

Fresh black pepper to taste

½ preserved lemon, chopped (optional) (see recipe)

1. Brown the onion in the oil in a heavy dutch oven or casserole.
2. Push the onion aside, add the meat and brown it on all sides. Add the garlic and sauté quickly.
3. Add the beans with the liquid they soaked in, add the tomatoes with their liquid, ½ a cup of the cilantro, the turmeric, salt and pepper.
4. Bring to a boil and let simmer, partially covered, until the liquid is absorbed and the beans are tender, for about 3 to 4 hours.
5. Before serving, stir in the remaining ½ a cup of cilantro and the preserved lemon, if desired. Heat through and serve. As a leftover, this dish reheats very well; it is also delicious when eaten cold.
6. Sprinkle with ½ a cup chopped fresh cilantro to garnish.

SPANISH RICE WITH SAFFRON

SERVES 6-8

1 tbsp oil

1 cup long-grain rice

1 onion, peeled and chopped fine

2 stalks celery with leaves, chopped fine

½ large or 1 small green pepper, seeded and chopped fine

1 clove garlic, minced

½ cup parsley, chopped

2–3 fresh tomatoes or one 8oz (225g) can Italian plum tomatoes with liquid

½ tsp saffron leaves

2 cups liquid, either water, chicken broth or the liquid from the canned tomatoes, or any mixture thereof

Coarse salt to taste

Fresh black pepper to taste

1. In a large skillet (pan or frying pan) with a tight-fitting lid, sauté the onion, celery, pepper and garlic in the oil until crisp tender. Drain the vegetables and set aside.
2. Add the rice to the skillet. Sauté, stirring, until the rice turns opaque. Meanwhile, bring the 2 cups of liquid to a boil in a separate saucepan.
3. Put the vegetables back into the skillet with the rice, and add the boiling liquid.
4. Add the parsley, saffron, salt and pepper to taste. Cover the skillet tightly and allow the rice to simmer for 15 minutes, or until tender.

COUSCOUS

When Grandma Elmaleh first came to America, pre-packaged couscous was unavailable in food markets, so she continued the tradition of making her own at home. This was a tedious, painstaking process of sprinkling quantities of semolina flour alternately with drops of salted water into a wide, wooden bowl, and then rubbing the two ingredients together briskly so that tiny little grains would form. These tiny morsels had to be deftly sifted and re-sifted so that the larger grains would separate out from the smaller ones. With the tiniest couscous grains, Grandma especially liked to prepare *brkooks* — a simple hot cereal dish made by tossing the steamed grains with butter and sour cream (or crème fraiche, if available) to taste. The rest of the couscous went into more elaborate recipes such as the following one.

Happily, nowadays we have the convenience of buying ready-made packaged couscous in many gourmet shops and supermarkets; it delivers a perfectly good result when prepared according to package directions.

COUSCOUS WITH CHICKPEAS

SERVES 6-8

½ lb (225 g) couscous
1 tbsp oil or butter
1 lg can chickpeas, drained
Chicken broth

1. Prepare the couscous according to package directions, substituting chicken broth for all or part of the water required.
2. 5 minutes before serving time, stir in the drained chickpeas and heat through.

chickpeas

CHICKPEAS

The very first 'movie theater' in Mogador was owned by Monsieur Sandillon, a local grain merchant. It consisted of a cavernous warehouse with an earthen floor, and people simply sat on the large sacks of grain. At that time, the American cowboy star Tom Mix was a favorite.
The audiences, both young and old were very animated and demonstrative. They would hoot and holler at the screen to warn Tom Mix whenever the bad guys were sneaking up on him… they actually believed the celluloid images could hear them. And when a villain did appear, the audience would pelt him with handfuls of dried chickpeas.

Here is a far more delicious way to use chickpeas:

RICE WITH CHICKPEAS

SERVES 6

1 cup rice
1 tbsp oil or butter
1 cup water
2 cups beef broth
1 can chickpeas, drained

1. Prepare the rice according to package directions, substituting the 3 cups of water with 1 cup of water plus the 2 cups of beef broth.
2. 5 minutes before serving, stir in the chickpeas and heat through.

SWEET-POTATO CHIPS
(Batata Mkhlia)

SERVES 4-6

3 sweet potatoes or yams, peeled and sliced 1/8"
   or thinner

Deep oil for frying

Coarse salt to taste

1. Heat the oil for deep frying in a wide skillet (pan or frying pan).
2. Pat the potato slices very dry with a paper towel.
3. Fry them in the oil one layer at a time. When golden, quickly remove them to a layer of paper towels to drain.
4. Serve them hot and crispy, sprinkled with coarse salt.

* * * * * * * * *

CRISP ROASTED POTATOES
(Batata)

SERVES 8

8 medium potatoes, peeled

Water to cover

¼ cup oil

Coarse salt

Paprika

1. Preheat oven to 350°F.
2. Parboil the potatoes in boiling salted water until tender on the outside but still firm on the inside. Drain them.
3. Coat the potatoes with oil and place them in one layer in a shallow baking dish. Sprinkle them with coarse salt and paprika to taste.
4. Bake them for 30 minutes or more until golden crisp on the outside and tender on the inside.

FISH DISHES

... Essaouira, seen from the old Portuguese fort, shines like a jewel in the Atlantic ...

The picturesque seaport of Mogador, now called Essaouira, was in past centuries the largest fishing and trading port in North Africa. Its strategic location between continental Africa and the Straits of Gibraltar, the gateway to the Mediterranean, was so important that for several centuries the Portuguese held it as a fortress and they built enormous crenellated ramparts all around the white-washed city, with look-out towers and rows upon rows of ornately scrolled cannon, which remain to this day, still bearing the emblem of Philip VI of Spain.

The sea was and still is the lifeblood of Essaouira. My grandmother, my mother, my aunt, uncles, great-aunts and great-uncles all spent their youth playing at *la sqala*, the name of that fortress on the rocky Atlantic Coast. Their soccer games at the beach, baking in the sun, plus liberal doses of fish liver oil, is what kept them healthy enough to survive the often bone-chilling damp sea air, windy and turbulent weather. My grandfather's daily constitutional consisted of a two-mile walk along the sand between his office and his home.

To see the bustling harbour of Essaouira as it is today, with its colorful fishing boats teeming with sardines shimmering silvery in the sunlight, against the ancient backdrop of stone walls, turrets and Moorish archways, is to understand why that city has produced such a wealth of seafood specialties all originating from the cultures of previous centuries.

Some of these treasures are preserved on the following pages.

DEEP-FRIED SMELTS WITH GRANDMA'S CHARISSA SAUCE
(El Hut Mkhli)

In Mogador, fresh sardines were plentiful and they were often prepared the following way. If you can't obtain fresh, fat, saltwater sardines, you could substitute smelts, a freshwater fish.

SERVES 4

1 lb (450 g) smelts, cleaned, with innards removed, heads and tails intact

Coarse salt to taste

Fresh black pepper to taste

1 cup flour

Oil for deep frying

Grandma's *Charissa* sauce (see recipe)

Lemon wedges to garnish

1. Rinse off the fish and dry in a paper towel. Spread them out on a piece of waxed paper and sprinkle liberally with coarse salt and pepper.
2. Dredge the fish with flour and coat them well.
3. Meanwhile, in a deep skillet (pan or frying pan) heat about 1½ – 2 inches of oil. When it begins to shiver (about 375°F), dust a little more flour on the fish, shake it off, and begin adding fish to the skillet, spreading them in one layer. Do not fry too many at once or it will reduce the heat of the oil. Turn them as necessary.
4. As the fish turn golden brown (it takes just a few minutes), remove them with a slotted spoon and drain them on several thicknesses of paper towels. Continue frying the remaining fish.
5. They can be re-warmed in a slow oven (200°F) until serving time. To serve, sprinkle the fish with a little extra coarse salt, if desired, and serve the lemon wedges and *charissa* sauce on the side.

MOROCCAN STRIPED BASS WITH CUMIN

Moroccans prepare this dish with a fish called *el buri*. It is not easy to find outside North Africa, but striped bass is very similar to it in texture and flavor. I have also used salmon, with excellent results.

SERVES 6 as a main course
SERVES 8–10 as an appetizer

One 5–6 lb (2.25-2.7 kg) of striped bass, scaled, innards removed, head and tail intact

Coarse salt

½ cup oil

3 tbsp ground cumin

1 tbsp paprika

1–2 cloves garlic, minced

½ cup parsley, chopped

Black pepper

1 lemon, sliced thin and seeded

3 carrots, peeled and cut into matchsticks

1 green pepper, sliced in ¼" strips

½ lb green beans, ends trimmed off (optional)

3 potatoes, peeled and cut in ⅛ths (optional)

1. Preheat oven to 350°F.
2. Rub the fish generously inside and out with coarse salt and let stand for 15 minutes.
3. Rinse the fish well.
4. Combine the oil, cumin, paprika, garlic, parsley, salt and pepper.
5. Lay the fish on a sheet of heavy-duty aluminum foil large enough to enclose the fish. Rub the fish inside and out with the spice mixture. Arrange the vegetable strips and lemon slices decoratively all over and around the fish. Wrap all tightly in the foil.
6. Bake the fish at 350°F for 1½ hours or until the fish is tender when tested with a fork. Open the foil during the last 15 minutes of baking.
7. Remove the fish, vegetables and gravy to a large oval serving platter, without disturbing the vegetable 'decoration' of the fish. Slice and serve.

BAKED STRIPED BASS WITH OLIVES AND LEMON
(El Hut Zitoun)

2 lbs (900 g) already cured green Spanish olives, pitted

1 tsp turmeric

1 tsp salt

Water to cover

5 lb (2.25 kg) striped bass, head and tail removed

1 preserved lemon, chopped fine

5 cloves garlic, minced

½ tsp turmeric

4 tbsps oil

½ cup water

Coarse salt

1. In a saucepan, bring the olives to a boil with the turmeric, salt and water to cover. Discard the water. Preheat the oven to 350°F.
2. Squeeze the cooked olives in paper toweling until all the water comes out of them.
3. Rinse off the fish, salt it liberally and let it stand for 15 minutes. Rinse it off again and place it in a baking platter with the lemon, garlic, turmeric, oil, water and salt if necessary. Smear the fish well with this mixture.
4. Add the olives all around the fish. Cover the fish with foil and bake it at 350°F for 1 hour.

* * * * * * * * *

FISH TAGINE WITH OLIVES AND LEMON

Proceed in the same manner as for the Baked Striped Bass with Olives and Lemon (see recipe). After step 2, rinse the fish, salt it for 15 minutes and rinse it off again. Cut the fish into slices 1-inch thick. Make a layer of all the olives in the bottom of a wide, heavy saucepan, and place the fish slices on top. Add the lemon, garlic, turmeric, oil, water and extra salt. Bring this mixture to a boil and let it simmer, covered, until the fish becomes tender and flaky when touched with a fork.

BAKED BLUEFISH WITH OLIVES AND PRESERVED LEMON

SERVES 4

One 5–6 lb (2.25 - 2.7 kg) bluefish, scaled, cleaned, innards removed, head and tail intact.

Coarse salt

¼ cup oil

3 wedges <u>preserved lemon</u> (see recipe)

2 cloves garlic, minced

1 tbsp <u>saffron water</u> (see recipe)

Coarse salt to taste

Fresh black pepper to taste

2 cups large already cured green Spanish olives, pits removed

1. Sprinkle the fish with coarse salt inside and out. Allow it to stand for 15 minutes, then rinse it in cold water thoroughly. Pat dry with paper towels.
2. Coat the fish with the oil and place it in a long baking dish.
3. Mince 2 wedges of the preserved lemon and blend it together with the garlic. Rub this mixture all over the fish, inside and outside.
4. Sprinkle the fish with salt, pepper and paprika to taste.
5. Sprinkle with saffron water.
6. Mince the third wedge of preserved lemon and place it inside the cavity of the fish.
7. Distribute the olives all around, inside and out.
8. Bake the fish at 350°F uncovered, for 1 to 1½ hours, depending on its size and thickness.

❊ ❊ ❊ ❊ ❊ ❊ ❊ ❊

BAKED FISH WITH CILANTRO (CORIANDER)

Follow the same recipe as the <u>Baked Bluefish with Olives and Preserved Lemon</u> (see recipe), except substitute 1 cup of minced fresh cilantro leaves (also called coriander or Chinese parsley) for the olives. Rub it all over the fish, inside and out. It will give this dish a completely different flavor.

DEEP-FRIED BLUEFISH WITH GRANDMA'S CHARISSA SAUCE

SERVES 4-6

One 5–6 lb (2.25 - 2.7 kg) bluefish, scaled, cleaned, innards removed, head and tail intact.

Coarse salt

Flour for dredging

Deep oil for frying

Grandma's *Charissa* Sauce for fish (*charissa*):

1 tsp paprika

1 dash cayenne pepper, or more, to taste

1 tsp ground cumin

2 cloves garlic, minced

2 tbsps oil

¼ cup vinegar (or lemon juice)

Coarse salt to taste

1. Sprinkle fish with coarse salt and let stand for 15 minutes. Rinse well and pat dry with paper towels.
2. Slice the fish crosswise into 1 inch thick slices.
3. Dredge the slices in the flour, coating well.
4. Fry the slices in the hot oil until they are crisp and golden on both sides. Drain the excess oil onto paper toweling.
5. Assemble the remaining ingredients. Blend together well and serve on the side as a sauce.

The following are customarily served as the fish course prior to the Passover Seder meal. It is a Sephardic version of the more eastern European *gefilte* fish. Brimming with tomato sauce, these savoury fish balls are well worth the effort any time of the year.

MOROCCAN FISH BALLS
(Albondigas de Pescado)

Makes about 2½ dozen
SERVES 10-12

2½ lbs (1.125 kg) haddock, halibut or turbot, or
    any white fish fillets, fresh or frozen (and thawed)

2 medium onions, coarsely chopped

1 cup parsley, chopped

1 egg

Coarse salt to taste

Fresh black pepper to taste

¾ – 1 cup matzo meal or cracker meal

One 16oz (450 g) can plum tomatoes, with liquid

2 cloves garlic, minced

1 tbsp oil

4–5 stalks celery, with leaves, cut into 3" lengths

½ cup parsley, minced

1 tsp sugar (optional)

½ cup water

1 cup tomato juice

Credit for this recipe must go to Mama Clara, my uncle Albert's grandmother, who brought this Portuguese treat from her home in Gibraltar many years ago.

1. Grind together in a meat grinder the fish, onions and parsley. Place the mixture in a large bowl.
2. Mix in the egg, salt and pepper, and the matzo meal. Use hands to blend it well and to shape balls about 1½ inch in diameter. Set the fish balls aside to 'fluff up' while assembling the sauce ingredients.
3. Prepare the sauce by bringing all of the remaining ingredients to a boil in a large kettle (pot). Add salt and pepper to taste. Drop in the fish balls very gently, and try to submerge most of the balls into the liquid.
4. Simmer all for 2–3 hours uncovered. The sauce will thicken slightly. These can be reheated just prior to serving either on top of the stove or in a 350°F oven for 30 minutes. Serve the fish balls over white rice, if desired. Any leftovers may be frozen.

DEEP-FRIED WHITE FISH FILLETS

Crispy on the outside, moist and succulent on the inside, these delectable morsels are even better served with the recipe for <u>Tangy Caper Sauce</u> (see recipe).

SERVES 6

2–3 lbs (900 - 1.350 g) fillets of any white fish, such as halibut, sole, flounder, etc. (This fish may be bought frozen in boxes and prepared while frozen, by slicing the 'blocks' of fish into 1½" thick slices; the fish 'cakes' will hold their shape beautifully throughout the frying.)

Coarse salt

Flour for dredging, mixed with a little salt and pepper to taste

Deep oil for frying

2 eggs, lightly beaten

2 tbsps minced parsley

<u>Caper mayonnaise</u> (see recipe)

1. If using fresh fillets, salt them and allow them to stand for 15 minutes. Rinse them well and pat dry with paper towels.
2. Heat the deep oil in a large skillet, pan or frying pan. An electric skillet works very well for this recipe.
3. Dip the fillets (or frozen fish 'blocks') into the flour mixture, coating them well, and deep-fry them on all sides. Handle them gingerly because they are fragile. When they are golden, remove them to paper toweling to drain.
4. Beat the eggs lightly in a shallow bowl, and stir in the parsley. Dip each piece of fried fish into this egg mixture, and then fry each piece in the oil a second time.
5. Serve the fish warm with caper mayonnaise. This and other fried fish recipes may be made entirely in advance and then reheated in a 350°F oven 30 minutes prior to serving time.

What to do with leftover fish? Work a little sorcery with —

CRISPY FISH CROQUETTES
(*Kefta del Hut*)

SERVES 4-6

3 cups leftover baked fish, such as striped bass or salmon, finely shredded, with all bones removed.

½ cup matzo meal

1 onion, peeled and grated

1 tbsp parsley, minced

Coarse salt to taste

Fresh black pepper to taste

1–2 eggs, lightly beaten

Deep oil for frying

Lemon wedges to garnish

1. Mash the first 7 ingredients together well with a fork.
2. Form the mixture into patties 2 inches in diameter, and deep-fry them in the hot oil. An electric skillet (pan or frying pan) works well for this recipe.
3. Drain them on paper toweling and serve them with lemon wedges.

MOROCCAN FISH SOUFFLÉ
(Ahammar)

For a festive luncheon entrée, make this soufflé. The peas, carrots and parsley give a confetti-like sprinkling of color to this molded fish dish.

SERVES 4-6

Two 7oz (200 g) cans tuna or salmon, or equivalent amount of leftover cooked white fish

2 cups mashed potatoes

1 small onion, peeled and minced or grated
    1 lemon, peeled, seeded and chopped fine or

1 preserved lemon (see recipe), minced

2 cups leftover peas and carrots (optional)

½ cup parsley, minced

4 eggs, separated, at room temperature

1. Preheat the oven to 350°F.
2. Grease a 1 quart baking dish.
3. Mix the fish, potatoes, parsley, onion, lemon, peas and carrots together.
4. Stir in the egg yolks and blend well.
5. Put the greased casserole dish into the oven to heat up a bit.
6. Beat the egg whites until stiff peaks form.
7. Fold the whites into the fish mixture very gently so as not to break the whites.
8. Pour all into the baking dish. Bake in the oven 25–30 minutes, or until a toothpick inserted comes out clean. Run a knife around the edges to loosen the soufflé, unmold it gingerly onto a platter and slice it into wedges to serve. This can be served with warm Tomato Sauce on the side (see recipe).

Like strawberries and fresh asparagus, shad and shad roe are true harbingers of spring. When April comes around, try this duet of shad recipes:

DEEP-FRIED SHAD WITH GRANDMA'S CHARISSA SAUCE.

SERVES 4

2–3 lbs (900 g - 1.350 kg) shad fillets
Coarse salt
Flour for dredging
Oil for deep-frying
Grandma's <u>Charissa sauce</u> for fish (see recipe)

1. Salt the fish well. Allow it to stand for 15 minutes, then rinse well and pat dry.
2. Dip the fish in the flour, coating well. Heat the oil for deep-frying.
3. Fry the fish until golden on both sides.
4. Remove the fillets to paper toweling to drain.
5. Serve warm with the *Charrisa* sauce.

* * * * * * * * *

SHAD ROE TAGINE WITH CILANTRO (CORIANDER)

SERVES 6

3 pairs shad roe
Coarse salt
½ tsp paprika
Dash cayenne
1 clove garlic, minced
2 wedges <u>preserved lemon</u>, (see recipe) minced
½ cup fresh cilantro (coriander) leaves, minced
½ cup water
2 tbsps oil

1. Sprinkle the roe with coarse salt. Allow to stand for 15 minutes. Rinse them well and pat dry.
2. Place them in a medium saucepan with the remaining ingredients.
3. Bring all to a boil and then simmer, uncovered, until the water evaporates and only the oil remains, as a sauce.

SARDINES À LA MOGADOR

For centuries, sardines have been the mainstay of the seaport of Mogador. Essaouira is, to this day, an enchanted world, a whitewashed fortress city jutting out into the turquoise Atlantic, virtually bypassed by twentieth-century progress. One can still go down to its primitive port and sample the fattest and freshest sardines in the world for just a few pennies. Accompanied by hot, crusty Arab bread, and sprinkled with fresh lemon, the fresh-caught grilled sardines are the best lunch I have ever had.

SERVES 4

2 lbs (900 g) fresh sardines, cleaned,
    innards removed

Coarse salt

Flour for dredging

Oil for deep-frying

Grandma's *Charissa* sauce for fish (see recipe)
    or lemon wedges

1. Salt the fish and allow them to stand for 15 minutes. Rinse them well and pat dry.
2. One by one, press each fish up and down its backbone, until the bone loosens up. Then the bone can be lifted out easily. Without this bone, the fish will lie very flat.
3. Press two sardines together, head to head and belly to belly. (The Arabs call this 'marrying' the fish.)
4. Dip them two by two into the flour. Heat the oil for deep-frying.
5. Deep-fry them until they are crisp on both sides. Drain them on paper toweling.
6. Serve the sardines with the Grandma's *Charissa* Sauce, (see recipe) or have each person assemble their own in the following delicious lunch.

PORT OF MOGADOR SARDINE SANDWICHES

SERVES 4

1 recipe <u>deep-fried sardines</u> (see recipe) served hot,
   or, if unavailable, use tinned sardines with a little
   of their oil to moisten the bread.

Coarse salt to taste

1 lemon, sliced into wedges

1 Bermuda Onion, sliced thin

Fresh Arab bread or whole wheat pita pockets,
   warmed in the oven.

1. Arrange the above items in separate platters and allow each person to assemble their own hot sandwich, layering the sardines and onion as desired, then sprinkling all over with lemon juice and coarse salt to taste. This replicates the way the sardines are served by Arab seamen on the wharves near their colorful fishing boats.

HOMEMADE PROVISIONS FOR THE JOURNEY TO MARRAKESH

When Grandma Elmaleh was a girl, it was her family's custom to escape the bleak seaside winters with a month-long vacation in the sun-baked desert oasis of Marrakesh.

The journey of 171 kilometers took them four days and three nights via a caravan of mules. Preparations for the voyage, called *L'Aween*, would begin a week in advance with the curing of fish, smoking of sausages and baking of biscuits — foods which required no refrigeration en route.

Each mule was laden with a rattan saddle, called a *chouari*, which had a large basket built in on either side. The baskets contained specially fitted wooden crates into which the provisions were packed. A mattress for sleeping was strapped on top of the *chouari* to make a more comfortable seat, and this was, in turn, covered by a rug. Grandma would thus sit astride the mule.

As there were no clocks, time was measured only by the position of the sun. At sunset, the caravan would stop and bed down for the night. Arab families living along the way were rightly known for their gracious hospitality. They would open their homes, no matter how humble, and gladly offer shelter to the travelers. They offered them the customary *senniah* — the brass tray laden with shimmering tea glasses and a teapot. A kettle of boiling water and sprigs of fresh mint would complete the welcoming tea ceremony. The visitors, in turn, would share their provisions with their hosts. They would unpack their *khleh* — the aforementioned crunchy beef nuggets, various cured olives, smoked sausages, and *chermilla*, chunks of bluefish marinated in a hot sauce. These foods were accompanied by *l'kak*, a sort of all-purpose yeast biscuit shaped like a doughnut. Hundreds of these were made in advance to last for the whole trip; they served as both bread and as tea cakes. After the meal, Grandma's family was provided with a basin of fresh cold water to wash off with and some floor space on which to spread their mattresses.

At bedtime, the Arab men would place long sticks outside their homes as a symbol of God's protection of their guests.

Next morning, the travelers were generously provided with fresh milk, eggs for the breakfast and boiling water for coffee or tea. After many thank-yous and *salaams*, the family would continue on its bumpy journey.

Once Marrakesh was reached, there were neither restaurants nor hotels. It was mandatory to rely on the hospitality of friends and relatives. Of course the only acceptable payment for this generosity was to reciprocate, which usually meant inviting the Marrakesh contingent to cool off in Mogador the following summer.

Herewith the recipe for *Chermilla* which was stored in airtight jars:

PIQUANT CONSERVE OF BLUEFISH
(*Chermilla*)

Two 5–6 lb (2.25 - 2.7 kg) bluefish, cut into
  3"x3" chunks

Oil for deep frying

1 tbsp cayenne pepper, or to taste – be careful

1 tbsp paprika

1 tbsp ground cumin

2 tbsps cilantro (coriander), minced

2–3 tbsps vinegar

Coarse salt to taste

1. Sprinkle the fish liberally with the coarse salt. Let it stand for 15 minutes, then rinse it off. Pat it dry with paper towels.

2. Heat the oil in a wide skillet, pan or frying pan. When it is very hot add the fish pieces and fry them on both sides until it is crispy on the outside and the skin turns very dark – almost black.

3. Remove the fish pieces to paper toweling to drain off excess oil.

4. Blend together the remaining ingredients and correct the seasoning to taste. Coat each piece of fish very well with this sauce and layer the coated pieces into an airtight container. Spoon the remaining sauce over all and close the lid tightly.

POULTRY
DISHES

POULTRY AND PRAYERS

While Grandma was raising her young brood in Mogador, there was an annual ritual that took place two nights before the High Holy Day of Yom Kippur. A rabbi would come to visit in the middle of the night with his lantern, and for every boy in the house he would slaughter one rooster, and for every girl he would slaughter one hen. He would then recite a prayer called the *Kapara*, and he would dab a drop of the sacrificial blood on each child's earlobe, as a blessing. Afterwards, the household would have so much poultry they would not know what to do with all of it. The servants would stay awake all night plucking those chickens, and one of Grandma's most vivid memories of the holidays was that of waking up to a kitchen full of feathers.

She recounts an anecdote in which her beloved Arab servant, Cabira, one year begged to be blessed alongside the children with the same *Kapara*, complaining that she needed some luck, as well. Lo and behold, three days later Cabira suddenly announced that she was engaged to be married. She credited the *Kapara* with bringing her the good fortune, but it was not so for Grandma. She thereby lost Cabira for good after twenty years of faithful service.

Feathers or not, poultry in any culture is still one of the most versatile of all foods.

ROAST CHICKEN À LA GRAMMIE
(Djaj M'Hammrin)

Sephardic as well as Ashkenazy Jewish families traditionally serve a simple roast chicken for Sabbath evening meal. The crackling golden skin and tender flesh produced by this recipe are nicely complemented by the following stuffings.

The credit must go to Grandma's mother, Simchah Levy, the grand lady who perfected this recipe.

SERVES 6

One 3 lb (1.350 kg) roasting chicken (reserve giblets for stuffing)

¼ lemon

1/3 cup oil

1 tsp garlic salt

1 tsp poultry herbs

1 tsp coarse salt

½ tsp fresh black pepper

1 tsp paprika

1 large onion, peeled and sliced into rings

1. Preheat the oven to 375°F.
2. Wash the chicken very well, inside and out. Rub it with the lemon wedge, squeezing the lemon juice all over. Reach between the skin and the flesh and remove any slimy membrane near the breast area. (Grammie always insisted that this was the source of a rather foul 'chicken smell'.)
3. Pour ½ of a cup water in a roasting pan. Coat the chicken with the oil and place it in the pan.
4. Rub the cavity of the chicken with the garlic salt and poultry herbs. Coat the skin with the salt, pepper and paprika. At this point, add the stuffing, if desired, and truss the opening.
5. Scatter the onions all over the chicken and place the pan in the oven. Bake for 1½ to 2 hours, basting it every 20 minutes or so. If the chicken gets too brown on top, cover it with a sheet of brown paper (make a 'tent' out of an opened out grocery bag) and continue to bake until tender.

CHICKEN WITH CILANTRO (CORIANDER) TAGINE

This is a delicious 'one-pot' dinner.

SERVES 6-8

2 chickens, quartered, well washed and rubbed
 with ¼ lemon

1 large onion, sliced

1 tsp coarse salt

2–3 cloves garlic, minced

½ tsp turmeric

2 tbsps oil

¼ cup fresh cilantro (coriander), chopped

1 lb (450 g) string beans, trimmed

6–8 new potatoes, unpeeled and halved

1. Place the chicken pieces in a pot with the onion, salt, garlic, oil, turmeric and cilantro. Add the string beans and the potatoes and toss lightly together in the seasonings.

2. Cover the pot tightly and cook over a very low fire.

3. The chicken, when cooked, will give off a lot of juice. Serve with extra bread for dunking.

CHICKEN FRICASSEE WITH MEATBALLS

The turmeric in this recipe turns the dish a lovely golden yellow.

SERVES 6

1 medium-sized chicken, cut into serving pieces
1 onion, sliced thin
3 cloves garlic, minced
½ cup fresh cilantro (coriander), minced
½ tsp turmeric
Coarse salt to taste
Fresh black pepper to taste
¼ cup oil
½ recipe for meatballs (as in Meatballs and Celery recipe)

1. Place the chicken pieces, onion, garlic, cilantro, spices and oil into a wide, heavy saucepan with a tight-fitting lid. Add ½ a cup of water.
2. Bring mixture to a boil and then lie the meatballs carefully into the juice in one layer.
3. Close the lid and let the ingredients cook on a very slow fire for 1 to 2 hours, or until the chicken is meltingly tender.

CHICKEN TAGINE WITH PRUNES AND ALMONDS

SERVES 4-6

One 3lb (1.350 kg) chicken, cut into serving pieces
¼ lemon
1 tsp coarse salt
Fresh black pepper to taste
2 cloves garlic, minced
¼ tsp turmeric
1 large onion, sliced
2 tbsps oil
8–10 prunes, pitted
½ cup blanched almonds
½ cup honey, or more, to taste

1. Wash the chicken very well. Rub it with the lemon wedge, squeezing the juice all over.
2. Place the chicken in a heavy pot and rub it all over with a little oil, the salt, pepper, turmeric and garlic.
3. Put the onion slices all over and add the remaining oil to the pot.
4. Cover the pot tightly and cook over a slow fire for 1½ to 2 hours.
5. 15 minutes before serving time, stir the almonds, prunes and honey into the chicken liquid. Heat through and serve.

GRAMMIE'S SUPERB ALMOND STUFFING

Makes enough to fill 2 large capons or a large turkey.

2 eggs, hard-boiled and minced

1½ cups seasoned breadcrumbs

1 cup chicken stock or bouillon

½ large onion, grated

2 stalks celery, with leaves, minced

2 large carrots, minced

½ large onion, minced

1 apple, peeled and minced

1 tbsp parsley, minced

1 tsp basil

1 tsp tarragon

1 tsp sage, crumbled

¼ tsp oregano

1 cup almonds, blanched (see procedure)

Coarse salt to taste

Fresh black pepper to taste

1½ tbsps oil

2 eggs

Enough matzo meal or cracker meal, as needed to bind

1 tbsp sugar, or to taste

1. Moisten the breadcrumbs with the chicken stock. Blend the minced egg, breadcrumbs and grated onion together in a bowl.
2. In a skillet (pan or frying pan), brown the grated onion, the carrots and the celery. Stir into the breadcrumbs mixture.
3. Stir in the herbs and the apple, blending well.
4. Blanch the almonds by placing them in a bowl and covering them with boiling water. Let the almonds soak a few minutes, then slip the skins off. Rinse the almonds and dry them. Then grind them in the grinder. Mix the almonds well with the stuffing.
5. Pass all of the stuffing through the grinder.
6. Add the oil and the eggs, and enough matzo meal to bind the stuffing. Taste and add sugar as desired. Blend well and allow to stand for 15 minutes, so that the matzo meal 'fluffs up'.
7. Stuff the bird(s) through the neck between the skin and flesh on the breast of the fowl. Put the remaining stuffing into the cavity(ies) and bake as directed.

CHESTNUT STUFFING

In place of the almonds, use 1 ½ cups of chestnuts, shelled and peeled, ¾ of them ground coarsely and ¼ of them left whole. Proceed as for Almond Stuffing (see recipe).

WALNUT STUFFING

Use 1 cup of walnuts in place of the almonds, and proceed as for Almond Stuffing (see recipe).

COUSCOUS AND RAISIN STUFFING

For 1 chicken or 3 Cornish hens

3 cups leftover cooked couscous
¾ cup raisins
½ cup chickpeas (if desired)
1 egg

1. Stir the above ingredients together.
2. Stuff into the cavity of the fowl and bake as directed.

GIBLET TAGINE WITH OLIVES AND LEMON

SERVES 6

1½ lbs (675 g) large already cured and pitted
  green olives

2–3 tbsps chicken fat

1 <u>preserved lemon</u> (see recipe), chopped

One 16 oz (450 g) can tomato juice

1½ lbs (675 g) chicken giblets (livers, gizzards,
  necks, etc.)

2–3 cloves garlic, minced

1 cup mushrooms, chopped coarsely

Coarse salt to taste

1 tsp turmeric

1. If using raw olives, pit them with a sharp, pointed knife. Bring them to a boil in water to cover with the salt and the fresh lemon (to prevent blackening). Discard the water, then repeat this process two or three times until the olives have lost their bitterness. Discard the water. (If using already-cured olives, omit this first step.)

2. Add the chicken fat to the olives. Add the preserved lemon, the garlic, giblets, mushrooms and enough tomato juice to cover all.

3. Season with coarse salt to taste, and add the turmeric.

4. Bring all to a boil and let simmer, partially covered, for 1½ to 2 hours or until the meat is tender and the tomato juice has reduced into a sauce.

GLAZED PIGEONS WITH CHERRIES

SERVES 4–8,
depending on size of fowl

4 pigeons or Cornish game hens, well-washed and
    rubbed with lemon
2 tbsps oil
1 large onion, peeled and sliced
¼ tsp saffron leaves or ½ tsp turmeric
Coarse salt to taste
Fresh black pepper to taste
¾ cup grape jelly
1 lb (450 g) mushrooms, sliced
¾ cup canned black cherries, drained

1. Preheat the oven to 350°F.
2. Heat the oil in a wide skillet, pan or frying pan,
    and brown the birds on all sides.
3. Season them all over with the saffron or turmeric,
    the salt and pepper.
4. Place them breast-side down in a large roasting
    pan. Add no water to the pan.
5. Bake them in the oven at 350°F until they get
    brown on top, for about 30 to 45 minutes.
    Keep checking.
6. Meanwhile, melt the jelly in a small, heavy
    saucepan over a slow fire until it liquefies a bit.
7. When the birds have browned on top, turn them
    over, breast-side up, and brush them with the
    melted jelly. Then sprinkle them liberally with the
    mushroom slices and the cherries.
8. Place them back in the oven and let them brown
    completely on the other side, for about another
    30 to 45 minutes. The birds will have made
    plenty of their own gravy.

SPICED MOROCCAN HENS
(T'njia)

This recipe adapts easily to larger quantities, and makes an especially impressive Moroccan-style party dish. This dish has always been a specialty of my grandmother's youngest sister, Lettie.

SERVES 6

3 Cornish hens
¼ lemon
Coarse salt
Fresh black pepper
½ cup olive oil (or other)
3–4 onions, sliced thin
½ tsp ground coriander
½ tsp ginger
½ tsp saffron
½ tsp cinnamon
½ tsp allspice
½ tsp nutmeg
½ tsp cloves (optional)
1½ cups water
½ cup raisins
1 cup honey
1 cup toasted blanched almonds

1. Wash the hens very well inside and out. Rub them with the lemon wedge, squeezing the juice all over. Sprinkle them with the salt and pepper.
2. Brown the onions in the oil in a wide, heavy enameled skillet (pan or frying pan). Keep stirring until they are all golden. Do not burn.
3. Preheat the oven to 350°F.
4. Blend all of the spices together, and rub them all over the birds, inside and out. Be generous with the spices, inasmuch as any leftovers will be added to the sauce.
5. Brown the birds on all sides in the same pan, pushing the onions to one side.
6. Add enough water to the pan to make a gravy and place the pan in the oven for I hour. So as not to over-brown the birds, cover them with foil for the first 30 minutes.
7. After the first 30 minutes, uncover the birds and add the raisins and the almonds. Then glaze the birds with some of the honey and add the rest to the sauce. Add water to the sauce if needed. Return the birds to bake for 30 minutes.
8. When they are golden and cooked through, halve each bird with poultry shears and serve on a platter with the gravy poured over. Serve with couscous.

HOMEMADE PHYLLO, ONE FRAGILE LEAF AT A TIME

When I was a little girl, I spent a lot of time in Grandma Elmaleh's kitchen. Indeed, it was the warmest, most fragrant and animated place in the entire house. I was most mesmerized by Grandma Elmaleh's procedure for making the flaky phyllo pastry leaves in the preparation of *pastilla*. It was far too complicated for two hands, so Grandma would enlist the help of her Moroccan housekeeper.

First, a quantity of flour was kneaded little by little with frequent sprinklings of water in a large bowl, until it formed a very loose and fluffy dough, which was almost like a thick paint. This was called the *warka*. Then the maid would heat a large Moroccan brass tray upside-down over a gas flame until it heated evenly all around. The back of this 'pan' was greased with a little oil and then wiped off immediately, whereupon quickly working fingertips would dab clumps of the dough all around the surface of the tray in a circular pattern. The thin residue of batter on the tray would 'melt' together to form one large sheet of pastry. When the pastry had dried slightly, it was peeled off and set aside under a damp towel and another sheet would be started.

Making a good-sized stack of these was a long, laborious, and enervating process, and Grandma, ever-resourceful, subsequently thought up a more practical method. Her invention was to thin the dough and paint it onto the hot tray using the widest-possible house-painting brush from the hardware store. This worked very well for many years, but even so, the leaves had to be used immediately or they would dry up, becoming too fragile and flaky to fold up.

Now, however, the advent of more ethnically oriented supermarkets has brought with it packaged frozen phyllo pastry leaves, which produce very successful recipes like the aforementioned *pastellitos* and the following *pastilla*.

FLAKY PIGEON PIE
(*Pastilla*)

Crackling, sweet and fragrant, this elaborate pastry is indeed the pièce de résistance of refined Moroccan cuisine. Traditionally, it is served whole as a communal appetizer and pieces are torn off and eaten by hand. Pastilla, however, makes an excellent main dish, sliced carefully into wedges. Each of its layers has its own distinct flavor; the tender poultry steeped in spices, then the lemony egg custard, followed by the crunchy sugared almonds and the crispy, gossamer pastry leaves.

SERVES 12

Two 2½ lb (1.125 kg) chickens, or equivalent amount of
   Cornish game hens, quartered, with giblets

1 tsp coarse salt

3 cloves garlic, peeled and minced

3 large onions, chopped

1 tsp fresh black pepper

1 tsp ginger

1 cup plus 1 tsp oil (sweet butter, melted, may be used
   if desired; this is the Arab method)

½ tsp leaf saffron

3 cups plus 1 tbsp water or chicken broth

2 tbsps plus 1½ tsps plus ¼ cup cinnamon

1 cup parsley, minced

¾ cup lemon juice

½ preserved lemon (see recipe), minced (optional)

1½ cups blanched almonds

8 eggs, lightly beaten

10–12 leaves of phyllo (or filo) pastry (about ¼ lb) thawed
   to room temperature*

¾ cup confectioners' 10x sugar

*This is available at many supermarkets in the frozen section, or at Greek or Middle Eastern specialty food shops.

1. Wash the poultry well and rub it inside and out with the coarse salt and the garlic. Allow the birds to stand for 30 minutes.

2. Rinse the poultry well. In a large pot, place the chicken, giblets, onions, pepper, ginger and half a cup of oil. Crumble the saffron leaves and add 2 tbsps cinnamon and the parsley.

3. Bring all to a boil. Then cover and simmer for 1 hour or until the chicken is tender and falling off the bones. Add the lemon juice.

4. In a separate skillet (pan or frying pan), heat 1 tsp oil and sauté the almonds until they are crunchy and golden. Drain them on paper towels. Chop them and then crush them a little finer with a rolling pin.

5. In a small bowl, mix the almonds with ¼ cup of the confectioners' sugar and 1½ tsps of the cinnamon. Set aside.

6. Strain all meat, giblets and loose bones from the pot. Bring the remaining sauce to a boil, uncovered, until it has reduced to about 1–¾ cups. Stir occasionally to prevent sticking.

7. Shred the poultry meat finely with the fingers, discarding all bones in the process. Chop the giblets finely and mix all the meat with ¾ of a cup of the reduced sauce. Set aside.

8. Stir the lightly beaten eggs into the remaining simmering sauce. Stir slowly and

steadily until the eggs set. Preserved lemon may be added at this point, if desired. Do not overcook or the eggs will become dried and crumbly. Set aside.

9. Preheat the oven to 425°F.

10. Unroll the pastry leaves gently, and keep a dampened towel over them to keep them from becoming too dry and flaky. On a baking sheet, pile 4 pastry leaves and bake them on a cookie sheet for just 40 seconds or so, just to crisp them.

11. Brush ½ a cup oil over the bottom and sides of a 12 inches round or 14 inches long oval baking pan which is 2 inches deep. Place one pastry leaf on the bottom, overhanging a few inches to one side, and place another leaf on top of that, overhanging a few inches on the other side.

12. Spread the egg custard over the pastry. Place the next few crisped leaves on top of that.

13. Spread the poultry mixture evenly over those leaves, and place the other 2 crisped leaves on top.

14. Now sprinkle the almond mixture all over the topmost layer.

15. Bring the bottom pastry overleaves up and fold them over the top, pressing them lightly into place. Place the remaining pastry leaves, unbaked this time, on the top of the pie, and fold all overhang under the entire pie, as if tucking bedsheets under a mattress.

Make sure that the pie is entirely sealed and that no fillings show.

16. Brush the entire pie with the remaining oil or butter.

17. Bake the pie at 425°F for 20 minutes, or until it is crispy and golden. With a long spatula pry the pie loose and invert it onto a cookie sheet or other shallow baking pan.

18. Place a serving platter over the pie and, holding firmly, invert it onto the platter.

19. Right before serving, dust the pie all over with the remaining ½ a cup of confectioners' sugar. Create a design on top of that with the cinnamon; place a stenciled pattern such as a doily or a star shape on top of the sugar layer and sift the cinnamon generously all over it. Or simply sprinkle the cinnamon with the fingertips, tracing a large cross-hatch pattern over the top. Serve the pastilla warm and crispy.

Note: This dish is best served freshly baked. Leftovers may be reheated, but the fillings are fragile and have a tendency to dry out the 'second time around'.

SWEET CINNAMON COUSCOUS
(Sfaa)

PUMPKIN SOUP WITH FRESH CILANTRO (CORIANDER) AND
ORANGE SALAD WITH POMEGRANATES

ORANGE AND OLIVE SALAD AND
PASTELLITOS

FISH TAGINE WITH OLIVES AND LEMON

SWEET MEATBALLS WITH PUMPKIN AND RAISINS

SESAME COOKIES
(Helwah d'Zinslan)

MEAT DISHES

CELEBRATING MEAT: GOOD TO THE LAST BONE

During the holiday seasons in Morocco, it was not uncommon for two or three families to get together to buy lambs and calves, slaughter them and share them among themselves. At celebrations, it was considered both proper and very generous to offer a live lamb or other livestock as a gift. Grandma recalled with amusement the bar mitzvah reception given in honour of her son Jacques. Every guest, upon arrival, was greeted with a chorus of 'yoo-yoos' by the other guests — shrill, ululating cries of good cheer. At one point in the party the 'yoo-yoos' became absolutely deafening. Grandma, entering the living room to see what all the commotion was about, was shocked to see a huge steer standing before her, bedecked with red ribbons on its horns. It was merely an extravagant gift from one of Grandpa's more well-to-do business associates.

It was always considered a sin to waste food in a Moroccan household. My mother distinctly remembers that as a young child whenever she would accidentally drop a piece of bread on the ground, one of the servants would scold her and tell her to pick it up and kiss it.

In a similar vein, Grandma also learned early to utilize every piece of an animal. With beef, for instance, the knuckles went into the weekly _Skhina_ (see recipe), tripes were cooked with hot pepper, bones went into soups, intestines were made into sausage casings, tongues were cured, and even the skins would be sent off to the local tannery to make decorative throw rugs for the house. The following chapter gives some of her ways to maximize the utilization of beef.

On the road between old Mogador and Marrakesh, there used to be a popular Sunday picnic ground called _le Quarante_, so named because it was exactly forty kilometres outside of town. Actually, it consisted of no more than an abandoned house by the roadside, surrounded by tangles of grapevines and a lone pomegranate tree, but it provided many families with a rustic enough retreat from the bustling 'city life' of Mogador.

At Grandma's childhood home, the picnic preparations would begin on the prior Saturday night, when the men of the family would head out to the _Quarante_ to dig a large hole in the earth to serve as a barbecue pit. They would fill it with coal and wood and ignite it with kerosene. When the pit became very hot, they would remove the fuel and the fire from it, and then they would suspend inside it a whole lamb — unseasoned, with innards removed — skewered on a long stick. The pit would be covered with a large basin that would then be weighted down on all sides to prevent the heat from escaping.

By noon the next day, the family would arrive with fresh picnic salads and tea things, and the men would then remove the 'all-night' barbecued *mechoui* onto a large serving tray for the family to pluck at with their fingers. Grandma Elmaleh fondly recollected how her mouth watered upon tasting the meltingly tender lamb chunks, dipped alternately into bowls of coarse salt, cumin seed and spicy *charissa* sauce.

LAMB ROAST
(Mechoui)

This Moroccan roast is crispy and spicy on the outside and meltingly tender on the inside. It is a spectacular entrée for a festive occasion, and it certainly feeds a crowd. At a lavish Moroccan celebration, a whole side of lamb is basted with the piquant <u>charissa sauce</u> (see recipe) and grilled outdoors on a barbecue spit. It is then served whole on a communal brass tray. The guests, sitting cross-legged on the floor, tear off chunks with their fingers and dip the lamb alternately into a small dish of ground cumin seed and a small dish of coarse salt.* Additional *charissa* may be served on the side. Those fortunate enough to have outdoor cooking facilities should by all means try a barbecue method. Otherwise, here is an oven-baked recipe which provides equally delicious results.

*It may be noted that etiquette requires that only three fingers of the right hand are used for eating. The left hand is reserved for hygienic purposes.

SERVES 8-12

¼ of a whole baby lamb
3–4 cloves garlic, minced
Coarse salt
<u>Grandma's *Charissa* sauce</u> (see recipe)
Cumin seed, ground

1. Preheat oven to 200°F.
2. Smear the lamb all over with the garlic and salt.
3. Place it in the oven in a large roasting pan. Leave it in the oven for 4 hours without opening the oven door.
4. After 4 hours, test it with a fork. If the lamb is tender, remove it from the oven. If not, shut the oven off and leave it inside for another 1 hour.
5. Serve warm with the *charissa sauce*, coarse salt and cumin seed on the side.

POTTED LAMB WITH WHITE TRUFFLES

Rare white truffles, indigenous to Moroccan soil, are a subtly-flavored relative of the darker, more pungent European variety. They can be found tinned at some gourmet shops. Truffles must be rinsed very well prior to cooking to remove any grittiness.

SERVES 6-8

1 small rack of lamb
2 cloves garlic, minced
Coarse salt to taste
1 can white truffles, drained and well-rinsed

1. Smear the lamb with the garlic and salt. Place in a pot without water and cover it tightly. Allow it to cook over a low fire until it is fork tender, for 2–3 hours.
2. After it has cooked, add the truffles into the cooking liquid.
3. Heat through and serve.

* * * * * * * * *

LAMB TAGINE WITH STRING BEANS AND LEMON

SERVES 6

1 small rack of lamb
2 cloves garlic, minced
Coarse salt to taste
1 lb (450 g) fresh string beans, washed and trimmed
½ lemon

1. Smear the lamb with the garlic and salt. Place in a pot without water, cover tightly and allow it to cook over a slow fire until it is tender, for 2–3 hours.
2. About 30 minutes before serving, add the string beans to the cooking liquid. Cook them until tender.
3. Sprinkle the dish with the juice of the lemon. Heat through and serve.

LAMB TAGINE WITH ARTICHOKES AND LEMON

Follow the previous recipe for <u>Lamb Tagine with String Beans</u> (see recipe), except substitute I can of artichoke hearts, drained. Cook them in the lamb gravy about 15 minutes before serving time. Then sprinkle with the juice of the lemon. Heat through and serve.

* * * * * * * *

ROAST LEG OF LAMB WITH CUMIN AND GARLIC

SERVES 6-8

1 whole leg of lamb, trimmed of excess fat
   and rinsed

2–3 garlic cloves, sliced into thin slivers

2 tbsps olive oil

1 tbsp ground cumin

1 tbsp rosemary, crumbled

1 tsp paprika

1 tsp coarse salt or more to taste

1 tsp fresh black pepper

Juice of ½ lemon

<u>Grandma's *Charissa* sauce</u> (see recipe)

1. Using a sharp, pointed knife, prick the lamb ½ inch deep in about twenty places all over the meat. Insert a sliver of the garlic into each slit.
2. Coat all of the meat with the olive oil.
3. Mix together the cumin, rosemary, paprika and black pepper, and coat the lamb with the mixture.
4. Allow the meat to marinate for several hours in the refrigerator. Before baking, smear the meat well with the lemon juice and the salt.
5. Bake at 350°F for 1½ hours or more, if necessary, until the lamb is tender but still pinkish inside. Lamb usually requires 25 minutes per pound. Serve the roast in thin slices with the *charissa* sauce on the side. Also, save the lamb bone for later use in soups.

My grandfather's good fortune in the business world started with his lucrative almond trade. Grown on beautiful white-flowering trees in the fertile Souss region of Morocco, the almonds were transported in great sacks across the backs of mules and camels to Grandpa's warehouse-office near the port.

My mother remembers how as a little girl, she and her brothers and sister would slide down mountains of the nuts and get covered with brown dust. The almonds were hand-shelled by veiled Arab women sitting cross-legged on the floor surrounded by various baskets. First they would pound them with stones to crack them open and then they would sort them according to size and quality. These would be bagged into 100lb burlap sacks and set out to line the streets, often stretching beyond the gates of the city. Then helpers would stitch the bags closed and the sacks would be loaded onto the backs of donkeys for the journey down to the docks.

Grandpa Elmaleh was nicknamed the 'Almond King', so it was fitting that his wife prepared some dishes which included these sweet, lovely nuts. Also see the recipe for sweet meatballs and the recipe for a moist, delicate almond cake.

LAMB TAGINE WITH PRUNES AND ALMONDS
(El Mrouzia)

SERVES 6

2 lbs lamb stew meat, cut into 1" cubes

Water to cover

2 cloves garlic, crushed

1 tsp coarse salt

3 tbsps oil

1 pkg pitted prunes

1 pkg (1 cup) whole blanched almonds

½ tsp cinnamon

½ tsp of *ras el hanout* – spice mixture sold in Moroccan spice stores.*

½ cup of honey, or to taste

1. Bring the lamb, garlic, coarse salt and oil to a boil in a pot with water to cover.
2. Simmer the lamb, partially covered, until the water reduces to about 1½ cups of sauce and the meat is very tender. This may take up to 2 hours of simmering.
3. Add the prunes, the almonds, the cinnamon, the *ras el hanout* and the honey, mixing them well with the lamb gravy. Make sure all the lamb chunks get coated well with this mixture. Correct the seasoning, heat through and serve. As is the case with many tagines, the leftovers taste even better.

* *Ras el Hanout* translates as 'head of the shop', referring to the individual shopkeeper's own special blend of spices. The mixture can be approximated from our own supermarket shelves by using:

black pepper	orris root	Blend a little of each according to personal taste.
cayenne	turmeric	
cinnamon	allspice	
cloves	coriander seeds	
ginger	cardamom	
mace	cumin seed	
nutmeg		

almonds

LAMB TAGINE WITH QUINCE AND ONIONS

SERVES 6

2 lbs (900 g) lamb stew meat, cut into 1" cubes
Water to cover
2 cloves garlic, crushed
1 tsp coarse salt
3 tbsps oil
4 quince, raw, peeled and quartered
2 onions, peeled and sliced into ½ circles

1. Bring the lamb, garlic, coarse salt and oil to boil in a pot with water to cover.
2. Simmer, partially covered, until the water reduces to about 1½ cups of sauce and the meat is very tender (up to 2 hours).
3. Remove the meat from the gravy. Set aside. Put the quince and the onions on the bottom of the pot, submerging in the sauce. Place the lamb back on top.
4. Cover the pot and simmer until the quince are tender, for about 30 minutes.

* * * * * * * * *

LAMB TAGINE WITH EGGPLANT (AUBERGINE)

SERVES 4-6

1–2 lbs (450 - 900 g) leftover cooked lamb roast, sliced ¼" thick
1 eggplant (aubergine)
Coarse salt
3 tbsps oil

1. Peel the eggplant in stripes. Slice it into ¼" thick discs, and sprinkle each of them with a little coarse salt. Layer the slices in a colander and allow them to 'sweat' for 30 minutes. They will release quite a bit of liquid, so dry them off with paper towels. (Discard the liquid.)
2. Heat the oil in a large skillet, pan or frying pan, and fry the eggplant slices on both sides until they are tender and golden.
3. Place the slices of meat on top of the eggplant, dot it with some of the frying oil, and heat it through over a low flame.

LAMBS' TONGUES

Tender and delicate, lambs tongues were served in the Elmaleh house during the Seder meal every Passover. They symbolize the head of the lamb, and the accompanying prayer is for God to 'put the Israelites at the head of their world and not at the tail'.

SERVES 6-8

1½ lbs (675 g) lambs' tongues (ordered from a butcher)

Water to cover

2 cloves garlic, crushed

1 tbsp oil

½ cup tomato juice

2 tsps ground cumin

Tomato sauce, optional (see recipe)

1. Bring the tongues and oil to boil in a pot with water to cover. Simmer, partially covered, until the tongues are tender and the sauce is reduced by about one third.
2. Peel off the tough outer skins of the tongues. Return to the sauce.
3. Add the tomato juice and the cumin. Taste to see if the sauce needs any extra salt (the tongues are naturally salty; they may not need any).
4. Simmer all together, uncovered, for an additional 30 minutes, or until the gravy thickens a little. Serve.

* * * * * * * * *

TOMATO SAUCE

This sauce has a bit more body and may be incorporated into the previous recipe.

3–4 large tomatoes, chopped

1 clove garlic, minced

1 tbsp oil

Coarse salt

½–¾ cup sauce from the lambs' tongues

1. Simmer the first 4 ingredients together in a saucepan until thick like jam.
2. Add the sauce from the lamb and heat the mixture through. Serve alongside the lamb.

BEEF

It must be noted that, with the exception of the filet mignon (Madame Elmaleh's variation on a Western theme) and the boiled meat in couscous, most of the following recipes call for ground beef. The beef indigenous to Morocco does not have the same tender consistency as that of the United States, thus Moroccans rarely eat steak or roast beef as we know it. Grilled or roast lamb is served in its place, while beef dishes comprise mostly meatballs, hamburgers (*kefta*), or meat fillings for pastries and vegetables. In fact the following dishes are not only savoury and exotic, they are also comparatively economical.

SWEET MEATBALLS WITH PUMPKIN AND RAISINS

Madame Elmaleh always served this as a sweet and spicy accompaniment for a vegetable couscous.

SERVES 6-8

1½ lbs (675 g) lean ground beef (such as ground round)

1 small onion, peeled and grated

2 tbsps parsley, minced

1 egg, lightly beaten

½ cup matzo meal, cracker meal or breadcrumbs

½ cup tomato juice

Coarse salt to taste

Fresh black pepper to taste

4 tbsps oil

6 onions, peeled and sliced thin

4 cups water

½ cup raisins, plumped in hot water to cover

½ cup prunes, pitted (optional)

1 cup blanched whole almonds

1 lb (450 g) sweet edible pumpkin or other orange squash, such as acorn or butternut squash, peeled, seeded and chopped into ½" cubes

½ –1 cup brown sugar or honey, according to sweetness desired

½ tsp ground cinnamon

1. Preheat oven to 350°F.
2. Put the meat in a large bowl with the grated onion, the parsley, egg and matzo meal. Blend well with the hands, and add tomato juice, salt and pepper. Knead well. Add 1 tbsp oil and knead again, until the mixture becomes a smooth paste.
3. Shape the mixture into small balls, about 1 inches in diameter. Allow the meatballs to stand for 15 minutes or so, while the matzo meal makes them 'fluff up' a bit.
4. In a large dutch oven, heat the remaining 3 tbsps oil. Cook the onions in the oil until tender and brown. Add the water and bring to a boil. Gently drop the meatballs one at a time into the simmering liquid. Simmer them uncovered until they are firm and the broth has reduced a bit.
5. Pour the meatballs and broth into a baking dish and add the drained raisins and prunes. Add the almonds and the pumpkin or squash, distributing everything evenly and arranging decoratively. Sprinkle all over with the cinnamon and the brown sugar or honey and bake until golden brown and some of the liquid evaporates, for about 1 to 1½ hours. Test the squash or pumpkin to make sure it is tender.
6. Serve on a bed of hot couscous, with the vegetables alongside.

GRANDMA'S MELT-IN-YOUR-MOUTH MEATBALLS AND CELERY
(*Krafs ouel Kouari*)

In the Elmaleh household, no Friday evening meal was complete without these aromatic, light-as-a-feather meatballs. Grandchildren (this one included) were known to fight over the cold leftovers for Saturday morning breakfast...

SERVES 6-8

1½ lbs (675 g) lean ground beef (such as ground round)

1 small onion, peeled and grated

1 egg

½ cup matzo meal or cracker meal

½ –1 tsp coarse salt (or to taste)

A liberal sprinkling of black pepper, or to taste (¼ tsp)

½ cup parsley, minced

½ cup tomato juice

¼ tsp ground cinnamon

¼ tsp ground nutmeg

¼ cup oil

1 tsp turmeric

1 bunch celery, washed and trimmed, outer stalks de-veined

3 cloves garlic, crushed

1. Put the meat in a large bowl with the grated onion, parsley, egg and matzo meal. Blend well with the hands, and add the tomato juice, cinnamon, nutmeg, and coarse salt to taste. Knead well. Add 1 tbsp oil and knead again, until the mixture becomes a smooth paste.*

2. Shape into balls 1½ inches in diameter, and set them aside for about 15 minutes, so that they fluff up a bit.

3. Cut the celery into 3 inches long strips. Place in a dutch oven with water to cover. Add 2 tbsps oil, coarse salt to taste, the turmeric and the garlic. Bring all to a boil, uncovered, until the celery is tender.

4. Drop the meatballs one by one into the cooking liquid. Partially cover the pot and simmer the meatballs for 2 to 3 hours, or until they are tender and the sauce has reduced to about 1 cup. Serve over rice or couscous.

*Madame Elmaleh often used a meat grinder to make this mixture as velvety smooth as possible.

MEATBALLS IN TOMATO SAUCE WITH ZUCCHINI (COURGETTES) AND PEPPERS

SERVES 6-8

1½ lbs (675 g) lean ground beef (such as ground round)

1 small onion, peeled and grated

½ cup parsley, minced

1 egg

½ –1 tsp coarse salt (or to taste)

Fresh black pepper to taste

½ cup matzo meal or cracker meal

1½ cups tomato juice

1 tsp ground cinnamon

½ tsp ground nutmeg

1 tbsp oil

1 green pepper, cored, and sliced into strips

1 red pepper, cored and sliced into strips

3 medium zucchini (courgettes), sliced into ¼" discs

2 cloves garlic, crushed

One 8 oz can tomato purée

1/8 tsp saffron leaves

½ cup parsley, minced

½ tsp crushed basil

1 bay leaf

Coarse salt to taste

1½ tsps sugar, or to taste

1. Put the meat in a large bowl with the onion, parsley, egg, salt and matzo meal. Blend well with the hands, and add ½ a cup of the tomato juice, cinnamon and nutmeg. Knead well until all the liquid is absorbed. Add 1 tbsp oil and knead again, until the mixture becomes a smooth paste.

2. Shape into balls 1½ inches in diameter, and set them aside for about 15 minutes so that they fluff up.

3. Put the peppers, garlic, tomatoes, tomato puree, saffron, parsley and 1 cup of tomato juice into a dutch oven. Add salt and pepper to taste. Bring all to a boil and if it is too tart add a little sugar to taste.

4. Gently drop the meatballs one at a time into the simmering liquid. Partially cover the pot and simmer the meatballs for 1½ – 2 hours, or until they are tender and the sauce has thickened a little. Serve over white rice or couscous.

FILET MIGNON WITH GRANDMA'S CHARISSA SAUCE

SERVES 6-8

1 filet mignon, 2½ lbs (1.125 kg) or so, trimmed of
  all excess fat

1 large onion, peeled and minced

1 cup parsley, minced

1 tsp coarse salt (or more, if needed)

1 tsp fresh ground black pepper

1 tsp paprika

2 tbsps oil

Grandma's *Charissa* sauce (see recipe)

1. Blend all the onion, parsley, salt, pepper and oil
   in a small bowl. Mix well.
2. Rub this marinade all over the meat and place it in
   the refrigerator to marinate for several hours
   or overnight.
3. One hour prior to serving time, place the meat
   under the broiler (grill) for 12 minutes on either
   side, to seize the juices and crisp the outside.
4. Turn the oven heat down to 350°F and bake the
   filet for an additional 20 minutes, so that the
   meat is pink and still juicy inside.
5. Serve in ½ inch thick slices with *charissa* sauce
   poured over.

* * * * * * * * *

BEEF BRISKET, SEPHARDIC STYLE

My grandmother often reminded me of the age-old wisdom that a good beef brisket, or pot roast
can only be made with a thick cut rather than a thin cut of beef. She was so right. A thin cut of
brisket results in a roast that is neither tender nor flavorful enough to please the palate.

SERVES 6

1 beef brisket, thick cut

Coarse salt

1 large onion, sliced

½ cup tomato juice

Horseradish (optional) or *charissa* sauce (see recipe)

1. Smear the brisket all over with coarse salt.
2. Place in a heavy pot, cover tightly and simmer over
   a very slow fire. Do not disturb or poke with a fork.
3. After 1½ hours, place the onion slices into the pot,
   and add the tomato juice to the gravy.
4. Cook for 30 minutes more or until all is tender.
   Serve with its own gravy, horseradish or *charissa*
   sauce if desired.

MOROCCAN HAMBURGERS (KEFTA) WITH ONION AND CILANTRO (CORIANDER)

SERVES 6

1 lb (450 g) lean ground beef (such as ground round)
¾ cup matzo meal, cracker meal or breadcrumbs
½ cup minced cilantro (coriander) or parsley
1 tsp coarse salt
½ tsp fresh ground black pepper
One 6oz can tomato juice
Grandma's _Charissa_ sauce (optional) (see recipe)

1. Assemble all the ingredients, except the _charissa_, in a large bowl. Knead together with the hands until well-blended.
2. Shape the meat into 6 patties and broil (grill), for 5–10 minutes on either side, or until they are done to taste.
3. Serve in warm Arab bread or in toasted pita pockets with _charissa_ sauce or ketchup, if preferred.

* * * * * * * * *

MOROCCAN HAMBURGERS (KEFTA) WITH GARLIC AND CUMIN

SERVES 6

1 lb (450 g) lean ground beef (such as ground round)
¾ cup matzo meal, cracker meal or breadcrumbs
1 tbsp ground cumin
1 tsp coarse salt or to taste
½ tsp fresh black pepper
One 6oz can tomato juice
1–2 cloves garlic, minced

1. Assemble all the ingredients in a large bowl. Knead together with the hands until well-blended.
2. Shape the meat into 6 patties and broil for 5–10 minutes on either side, or until they are done to taste.
3. Serve in warm Arab bread or toasted pita pockets with _charissa_ sauce, if desired, or ketchup.

A traditional couscous dinner is the showpiece of Moroccan cuisine. Couscous itself is a grain from semolina, but the term 'couscous' also means the elaborate feast which uses the bland cereal as a backdrop for myriad flavors, exotic textures and heady fragrances, from the sweetest to the hottest. For example, a couscous banquet might comprise:

PASTILLA
COUSCOUS WITH VEGETABLES AND BOILED BEEF
SWEET MEATBALLS WITH PUMPKIN AND RAISINS
PIQUANT TOMATO SALAD
ORANGE AND OLIVE SALAD
POMEGRANATE AND WALNUT SALAD
DATES STUFFED WITH ALMOND PASTE AND WALNUTS
FRESH MINT TEA

The intermingling of all these flavors and aromas can induce a reverie of dining in a sumptuous Moorish palace with a pasha or two.

Any leftover couscous can be re-steamed several times. A delicious 'morning-after' breakfast is *sfaa*, for which the steamed cereal is tossed with a little milk, butter, cinnamon and sugar to taste (see recipe).

COUSCOUS WITH VEGETABLES AND BOILED BEEF

SERVES 8-12

One 1lb (450 g) pack of couscous

One 3–4 lb (1.350-1.800 kg) breast of beef

Several cracked soup bones, preferably beef shin

4 carrots, peeled and cut into 3" lengths

6 onions, peeled and coarsely chopped

6 stalks celery, trimmed and cut into 3" lengths

6 or more small white turnips, peeled

½ lb (125 g) Swiss chard, well-washed and cut
   into 3" lengths

1 small pumpkin or large acorn squash, cut into
   2" hunks and seeded

1 bunch leeks, well-washed, trimmed and cut into
   3" lengths

One 8oz (225 g) can chickpeas, drained

1½ cups parsley or cilantro (coriander)

4 quarts water

Coarse salt to taste

Fresh black pepper to taste

COUSCOUS

1. Place the couscous into a basin and add enough cold water to cover. Stir well and drain off the excess water.

2. Place the meat, bones and all of the vegetables (except the chickpeas) with water, salt and pepper in the bottom of a couscous cooker (called a 'couscoussiere') or other large utensil for steaming and bring to a boil. Simmer, skimming the surface with a slotted spoon as necessary, for about 30 minutes.

3. Work the couscous with the fingers to break up any lumps. Moisten it with the stock from the boiling meat, then spoon the cereal into the top compartment of the steamer (lined with cheesecloth if the holes are too big). Place the couscous over the boiling meat and vegetables. Cover tightly and steam for 1 hour.

4. Pour the couscous back into the bowl. Add more broth to moisten it. Return the couscous to the steamer and cover tightly.

5. Add the chickpeas to the meat and vegetables in the bottom of the steamer. Steam everything for 1 more hour.

6. Serve the couscous cereal moistened with a little more soup stock, carefully moulding it into a cone shape on a large round serving platter. Serve the meat and the vegetables, both sprinkled with a little coarse salt, in accompanying serving platters.

DAFINA
(Shkhina)

According to Jewish law, Saturday is the Sabbath, when no work may be done. Therefore, in Mme. Elmaleh's household, Saturday's midday meal was often prepared a day in advance. The Eastern European Jews prepare a one-pot dish called *cholent* which is very similar in that they are both cooked overnight on Friday and then served after the synagogue services, around noon on Saturday. The Moroccan Jews, in a country only recently modernized, often sent their *dafinas* in their respective family's pots to the large community oven to bake overnight. It was not uncommon for the pots to get mixed up. Imagine how surprised one Jewish family was to receive another Spanish family's paella, chock full of such un-kosher tidbits as shrimp, clams and pork sausage.

Please note that this particular recipe feeds a regiment. The food sticks to the ribs and one feels 'full' for up to a week afterwards. The additional puddings and stuffings are sublime embellishments, especially when imbued overnight with the various meat gravies, but any of them may be omitted if desired. The components of this dish can be adjusted freely and served in any quantity or combination. One or two piquant salads provide a perfect counterpoint.

BASIC DAFINA

¼ cup oil

2 cans chickpeas, drained

1 bulb garlic, each clove peeled and left whole

1 tbsp coarse salt

1 tsp turmeric

One 4lb breast of beef, rubbed with coarse salt

8 calves' feet (available from a butcher)

2–3 cups beef fat, ground (to be used later in the
   puddings, if desired)

1 medium potato per person, peeled

1 medium sweet potato per person, peeled

1 egg per person, left raw in shell

OPTIONAL INGREDIENTS:

1 egg pudding (see recipe)

1 rice and bean pudding (see recipe)

1 meat-filled derma (see recipe)

1 wheat pudding (see recipe)

1 dark fruit pudding (see recipe)

1 boiled beef tongue (see recipe)

1. Assemble the oil, chickpeas, garlic, salt,
   turmeric, beef and calves' feet in the bottom of
   a large enameled pot.
2. Now begin making the puddings.
3. Place the puddings, securely wrapped in
   cheesecloth on top of the other ingredients.
   Fill the pot onto the top of the stove. (It is heavy
   and may require an extra pair of hands.) Bring
   the dafina to a boil.
4. When it has begun boiling, add the potatoes,
   the sweet potatoes and the eggs.
5. Allow the dafina to simmer, covered, on top of
   the stove for 4 to 5 hours.
6. Remove it from the stove and place it in a slow
   oven (200°F) overnight, until 12:00 the next
   day. (Early that next morning, check to see if it
   needs additional water. Add it, if necessary,
   and also add the previously boiled beef tongue,
   if desired.)
7. 30 minutes before serving, shell the eggs.
   They will be hard-cooked and brown from the
   beef juices. Put them back in the pot to keep
   warm.
8. Serve the meats, the potatoes, the eggs and
   the puddings each in separate platters.
   The remaining liquid is a very hearty beef broth
   which is ladled out either as a gravy or as a soup
   with the chickpeas.

EGG PUDDING

2 hard-boiled eggs, minced
½ cup ground beef fat
½ cup breadcrumbs
½ cup parsley, minced
½ tsp marjoram
2 raw eggs
Coarse salt to taste

1. Mix all the ingredients together. Set them aside to fluff up for 20 minutes.
2. Roll the pudding into a sausage shape.
3. Wrap securely in a double thickness of moistened cheesecloth.

* * * * * * * *

RICE AND BEAN PUDDING

1 large onion, minced
1½ cups rice, rinsed
Coarse salt to taste
Fresh black pepper to taste
¼ cup dried kidney beans
1 tbsp oil

1. Mix the ingredients together.
2. On a large double-thick square of cheesecloth, place the mixture in the center. Bring the four corners of the square together and tie the ends together with a piece of string to form a secure bag with plenty of room for the expansion of the beans and the rice.

MEAT STUFFING FOR DERMA
(El Enbar)

2 cups ground beef

1 small onion, minced

1 egg

½ cup parsley, minced

1 tbsp oil

¼ cup tomato juice

¼ cup matzo meal

½ cup raw rice, rinsed

1 length of *derma* (beef intestine – available from a butcher)

1. Mix all ingredients except the rice and the *derma* very well by hand until they form a smooth paste.
2. Mix in the ½ a cup of raw rice. Let the mixture stand for 20 minutes to fluff up.
3. Stuff the mixture into the piece of *derma* and secure with a piece of string at both ends.

* * * * * * * * *

WHEAT PUDDING

1½ cups whole grain wheat kernels

1 clove garlic, minced

1 tbsp oil

1 tsp ground cumin, or whole cumin seeds

Coarse salt to taste

1. Mix all ingredients together.
2. On a large double-thick square of moistened cheesecloth, place the mixture in the center. Bring the four corners of the square together and tie the ends together with a piece of string to form a secure bag with plenty of room for the expansion of the wheat.

DARK FRUIT PUDDING

This rich, fragrant dish bears more than a passing resemblance to what the English call 'plum pudding'. It may very well be a legacy from the English tradesmen who settled in Mogador in the nineteenth century.

2 large sweet potatoes, peeled and chopped into large hunks.

8 oz dark raisins

½ lb (225 g) beef fat

1 cup walnuts

1 piece of _mazhoun_ (preserved grapefruit) (see recipe)

½ cup matzo meal, cracker meal or breadcrumbs

¼ cup oil

1/3 cup brown sugar

2 tsps cinnamon

1 tsp cloves (optional)

2 eggs

1. Grind together the first 5 ingredients.
2. Mix them by hand with the remainder of the ingredients, blending all very well. Set the mixture aside to macerate and fluff up for about 20 minutes.
3. Roll the mixture into a 3 inch thick sausage shape, and place on a double thickness of moistened cheesecloth. Roll the ends up and tie securely at each end with a piece of string.

The following two recipes are Moroccan variations on a French dish known as 'parmentier', which is also related to an English 'shepherd's pie'.

NOODLE PASTEL WITH MIGA

SERVES 6-8

½ pkg thin egg noodles
½ stick margarine
2 eggs, slightly beaten
1 recipe *miga* meat filling (see recipe)
2 hard boiled eggs, sliced into wedges

1. Preheat the oven to 350°F.
2. Prepare the noodles according to package directions. Drain them well and toss them with the margarine and one beaten egg.
3. Grease an oven-proof casserole dish. Place half the noodles in the bottom, spreading them evenly and building them slightly around the sides of the dish.
4. Stir the other beaten egg into the *miga* mixture and blend well. Spread the *miga* evenly on top of the noodle layer. Smooth it out with a spatula.
5. Distribute the hard-boiled egg wedges all over the top and press them into the *miga* mixture.
6. Cover with the remaining noodles. Try to fill in any spaces so that the sides are 'sealed' and the meat filling does not show.
7. Put the casserole in the oven and bake at 350°F until the noodles turn golden and crunchy, for about 1½ hours.

POTATO PASTEL WITH MIGA

My grandmother was always the first to boast that she has kept up with the times and adapted her recipes to today's more modern shortcuts. Witness the following:

SERVES 6-8

½ large pkg potato buds (prepared according to package instructions, substituting margarine for butter, if desired) or equivalent amount of freshly mashed potatoes

2 eggs, slightly beaten

1 recipe _miga_ meat filling, or chicken miga filling (see recipe)

2 hard-boiled eggs, sliced into wedges

1. Preheat the oven to 350°F.
2. Stir one beaten egg into the potato mixture.
3. Grease an oven-proof casserole dish. Place half the potato mixture on the bottom, spreading it evenly with a spatula and building up an extra ½-inch up around the sides of the dish.
4. Stir the other beaten egg into the _miga_ mixture, blending well. Spread the _miga_ on top of the potatoes, smoothing the layer with a spatula.
5. Distribute the hard-boiled egg wedges evenly and press them into the _miga_ layer.
6. Cover with the remaining potatoes, smoothing them out with a spatula. Try to patch any spaces so that no meat filling shows.
7. Coat the palms with oil and smooth out the top layer of potato. Decorate the top by running the tines of a fork along the surface, making wavy lines, criss-cross designs or any decorative pattern. Any leftover potato mixture can be molded into little petals, leaves or ball shapes that can be pressed onto the middle or edges for the crust.
8. Bake at 350°F for 1½ hours, or until the casserole crust is golden.

DEEP-FRIED POTATO PASTELLITOS

6 large old potatoes, peeled and boiled with 1 tsp
  salt in water to cover

2 eggs, lightly beaten

2 tbsps matzo meal

1 recipe _miga_ meat filling (see recipe)

2 egg whites

Deep oil for frying

1. Boil the potatoes and then let them simmer uncovered over a slow fire until the water evaporates and the potatoes are very dry. Take care not to burn them.

2. Mash the potatoes adding the beaten eggs and salt to taste. Add enough matzo meal to bind the mixture a bit.

3. Coat the hands with oil. Into a handful of potato mixture, place about 2 tablespoonfuls of the _miga_ meat filling. Cover this with another layer of potato and mold into a completely sealed oval patty shape with no meat showing. Each _pastellito_ should be approximately 1½ inches wide and about 2 inches long. Continue in the same fashion until all potato and _miga_ is used up.

4. Heat the oil in a deep, wide skillet (pan or frying pan).

5. Meanwhile coat each of the patties with the egg white.

6. Drop the patties one by one into the skillet in one layer and keep turning them until they are golden brown on all sides.

7. When they are done, remove them to paper toweling to drain off any excess oil. They can be made in advance up to this point and then reheated in the oven, at 350°F for 30 minutes.

CHANGING TIMES

Refrigerators were non-existent in my grandmother's youth. *Trissinti*, the Arab word for electricity, did not become available until the 1930s, and even then it usually took the form of one dim, dangling light bulb straining to light the entire house. The telephone, or *tinifoor*, as it was called, came much later, and anyone who has had the experience of dialling in Morocco will vouch for the fact that the appliance has not improved much since. Anyhow, the only refrigerator, or *frigidir* in the Levy house was the cool stone stairway between the kitchen and the terrace (called the *spinza*). Otherwise, all perishable foods were shopped for on a daily basis at the local souk.

One method for prolonging the shelf life of meat was to smoke it. Grandma recalled making beef sausage by washing and 'blowing out' beef intestines to make casings for the ground, or rather pulverised, meat. First the meat was salted with saltpetre to retain its pink color, then the saltpetre was rinsed off. For lack of a grinder, the meat was pounded fine in a mortar with a pestle, with black pepper stirred in. Once the casings were stuffed, the sausages were hung with cords from the inside of a long, cylindrically shaped basket. A fire was kindled in a low-to-the-ground stove, then sawdust was sprinkled over the fire to cause it to smoulder. The basket with the sausages (and whatever meat or poultry that was on hand) was covered with thick burlap and set over the stove to smoke. This procedure would be repeated three to four times before the meat was properly cured. Grandma Elmaleh was always awed by the wide variety of pre-smoked sausages and pre-pickled tongues to be found ready-made in American supermarkets.

BOILED BEEF TONGUE (*El San*)

Well-prepared beef tongue is one delicacy which is all too often overlooked. Its texture is so soft and buttery that one scarcely needs a knife to cut it. Enhanced by a tangy 'chow-chow' (mustard pickle – another legacy of the British to Mogador) or one of the following sauces, its flavor is truly sublime.

SERVES 6

1 pickled beef tongue
Water to cover
1 bay leaf
1 large onion, sliced

1. In a large pot with water to cover, bring the tongue to a boil. Discard the water and repeat this process twice more with fresh water each time to get rid of the saltpetre in the tongue. Drain.
2. Put it in the pot with fresh water to cover, this time adding the bay leaf and the onion slices.
3. Bring it to a boil and let it simmer, uncovered, until it is soft and tender when tested with a fork.
4. Let the tongue cool slightly, then peel off the tough outer skin and serve the tongue sliced with mustard or one of the accompanying sauces.

RAISIN SAUCE FOR TONGUE

1 cup cooking liquid from tongue
½ cup raisins.

1. Put ingredients in a small saucepan and heat together uncovered, until the liquid reduces a bit and the raisins plump up.

LEMON CAPER SAUCE FOR TONGUE

2 egg yolks
2 tbsps water
2 tbsps lemon juice or vinegar
Coarse salt to taste
Fresh pepper to taste
2 tbsps tiny capers (if large, mince them)
1 hard-boiled egg, minced (optional)

1. Stir the yolks, water and lemon juice or vinegar in a small heavy saucepan over low heat until slightly thickened.
2. Stir in the capers, seasoning, and hard-boiled egg, if desired, and heat through. Cook for no more than 5 minutes or the sauce will curdle. Serve warm drizzled over sliced tongue.

Another sadly under-appreciated delicacy is calves' brains, with their silky, custard-like consistency and subtle flavor. My mother recalls how, as a schoolgirl in the French lycée in Casablanca, her classmates would feast on brains before an exam in hopes that it would make them smarter.

The following dishes are a good introduction to this delicious and surprisingly versatile food. (The trick is to divulge the ingredients only after the more squeamish eaters have cleaned their plates.) Leftover brains can also be incorporated into quiches and omelettes.

CALVES' BRAINS WITH CILANTRO (CORIANDER) AND PRESERVED LEMON
(Demagh)

SERVES 6

3 pairs calves' brains, well-washed, with outer membrane removed

1 tsp coarse salt

2 tbsps oil

½ tsp paprika

3 cloves garlic, minced

2 wedges <u>preserved lemon</u>, minced (see recipe)

½ cup fresh cilantro (coriander), chopped

1 cup water

Coarse salt to taste

1 egg per person, optional

1. In a large pot, bring the brains to a boil in water to cover. Discard the water and repeat this process two more times, using fresh water each time. On the third boiling, add the 1 teaspoonful coarse salt. Bring to a boil and drain.

2. Place the brains in a saucepan with the oil, paprika, garlic, preserved lemon, cilantro and water. Bring all to a boil and let simmer, partially covered, until the water has evaporated and only the oil remains as a sauce. Add coarse salt to taste.

3. If desired, 10 minutes before serving, gently drop the eggs one by one into the sauce with the brains and let them poach, covered, until serving.

DEEP-FRIED CALVES' BRAINS WITH TOMATO SAUCE

SERVES 4

2 pairs calves' brains, well-washed, with outer
   membranes removed

1 tsp coarse salt

Water to cover

1 egg, lightly beaten

1 tbsp parsley, minced

Flour for dredging

Oil for deep-frying

TOMATO SAUCE:

One 8oz (225 g) can Italian plum tomatoes, with liquid

2 cloves garlic, minced

1 tbsp oil

Coarse salt to taste

½ tsp sugar (optional)

1. In a large pot, bring the brains to a boil in water to cover. Discard the water and repeat this process twice more, using fresh water each time. On the third boiling, add the 1 teaspoonful of coarse salt to the water.

2. Bring the brains to a boil, then drain them.

3. Slice the brains into ½ inch thick slices. Pat them dry.

4. Heat the oil for deep-frying.

5. Beat the egg lightly with the parsley in a shallow bowl. Dip the slices first into the egg mixture, and then dredge them in the flour, coating them well.

6. Deep-fry the slices until they are crisp and golden on both sides. Remove them to paper toweling to drain.

7. Meanwhile, heat the tomatoes in their liquid with the garlic, oil, and coarse salt to taste. If the mixture is too acid-tasting, add the sugar. Bring the sauce to a boil and then simmer.

8. While the brains are still warm, stir them into the simmering tomato sauce and serve at once.

MOLDED BRAIN PATÉ

This crown-like mold ingeniously transforms any ordinary meat filling into a regal delicacy.

2 pairs of calves' brains, well-washed, with outer membranes removed

1 tbsp coarse salt

Water to cover

3 cups *miga* meat filling recipe or any other Moroccan stuffing recipe

Parsley sprigs to garnish

Tomato sauce (see recipe), optional

1. In a large saucepan, bring the brains to a boil in water to cover. Discard the water and repeat this process two more times, using fresh water each time. On the third boiling, add the 1 tablespoonful of coarse salt.
2. Preheat the oven to 350°F.
3. Drain off the liquid from the brains and slice them ¼-inch thick.
4. Line the bottom and sides of a well-greased medium-sized over-tempered glass bowl with the thin slices of brain, trying to cover the surface of the bowl completely and decoratively.
5. Fill the lined bowl with the meat filling and smooth out the top to make it level.
6. Bake the mold at 350°F for 1 hour.
7. Let it cool slightly, then gently run a sharp knife around the edge to loosen the mold. Turn it out onto a serving platter and garnish it with the parsley sprigs.
8. Slice the mold into wedges and serve it with warm tomato sauce on the side, if desired.

TRIPE À LA MAROCAINE
(Demagh)

SERVES 4

1 set of beef tripe (buy it partially pre-cooked)

Water to cover

½ cup oil

4 cloves garlic, minced

1 tsp salt coarse salt

Fresh black pepper to taste

1 cup tomato juice

A few hot pepper flakes, if desired

1 tsp cumin

1. Wash the tripe very well by pouring boiling water over them in a colander, until no brownness remains.
2. Cut them into 1-inch sections and place them in a saucepan with the remaining ingredients.
3. Bring the mixture to a boil, and let simmer, partially covered, until the tripe is tender, for about 30 minutes.

CONDIMENTS AND SAUCES

SAFFRON WATER

Saffron 'leaves' are an essential ingredient in the cuisines of Morocco, Spain and Portugal. The golden-red threads are actually the tiny pistils of the saffron flower, and the labour involved in harvesting them makes the spice very costly indeed. My grandmother used the spice very sparingly; in order to stretch its value, she would make an 'extract'. One tablespoonful of this saffron water is a sufficient substitute for the spice in most any recipe. Its flavor is just as potent, and the orange-colored liquid turns food just as golden. Try this in a chicken tagine or in a rice recipe.

1 tsp saffron 'leaves'
1 cup boiling water

1. Put the saffron leaves in a jar and pour the boiling water over them. The leaves will steep and the liquid will turn orange in color.
2. Let the liquid cool to room temperature, then store the jar in the refrigerator for future uses.

* * * * * * * * *

PRESERVED LEMONS
(Lima M'Tikha)

This 'pickling' process transforms ordinary lemons into soft, translucent delicacies with their own unique flavor and aroma. Grandma would make these two to four weeks ahead of time and she would always keep them on hand to flavor salads and tagines. I remember huge jars of them lining her pantry.

10–12 fresh lemons
Coarse salt
Mason jar(s) with tight-fitting lids, sterilized
Olive oil

1. On a cutting board, set each lemon one at a time on its flat stem end. With a sharp stainless steel knife, cut straight down through the center of each lemon to about ½ inch from the base. Do not sever completely. Make another slice

down the middle of the lemon, this time quartering it. Again do not slice all the way through.

2. Dip each lemon into coarse salt and put a pinch of salt down into the middle of each lemon. Press the quarters back into shape.

3. Make a layer of salt ¼ inch deep in the bottom of the mason jar(s).

4. Pack the lemons down into the jar(s). Make a layer of lemons then another sprinkling of salt, then more lemons. Push all the lemons down so that they fit snugly. They will leak their juice and this will rise to cover the lemons.

5. Fill the jar with about ½-inch layer of olive oil, then seal the jar.

6. Let the lemons stand in a cool dry place for at least 2 weeks, until the lemons are firm but tender and slightly translucent.

7. Always rinse off each piece of lemon before using it. After the jar has been opened, it is a good idea to store the remainder of lemons in the refrigerator.

MARINADE FOR BROILED (GRILLED) FISH, LAMB OR LIVER

Makes ½ cup

½ tsp paprika

½ tsp garlic powder

½ tsp ground cumin

1 tsp coarse salt

1 tbsp lemon juice (for fish) or 1 tbsp vinegar
  (for meat)

⅛ tsp cayenne pepper

1. Mix the above ingredients very well.
2. Rub the fish or meat very well with the mixture. Refrigerate the meat for several hours or at least let it stand for 15 minutes at room temperature to absorb the flavors.
3. Broil or grill the meat 10 minutes on either side, or until it is done to taste.

* * * * * * * *

GRANDMA ELMALEH'S CHARISSA SAUCE

This was Grandma's special sauce, a delicious condiment which combines the peppery heat (added to taste) of the traditional Moroccan Harissa hot pepper sauce, with the spicy cumin-and-garlic based Chermoula sauce used in this book's fish recipes. Hence the Elmaleh family's name for it: 'Charissa' Sauce. This sauce tastes great on almost anything: meat, fish, poultry, eggs, vegetables, chips, pita bread… discover your own favorite way to use it. It can be made to taste as mild or as piquant as desired, simply by adjusting the amount of cayenne pepper used.

Makes ½ – ¾ cup

1–2 garlic cloves, minced or crushed

1 tsp coarse salt (or to taste)

1 tbsp ground cumin, or whole cumin seeds, crushed in a mortar

2 tsps paprika

½ cup parsley, minced

⅛ tsp cayenne pepper, or to taste

1–2 tbsps lemon juice, or to taste

4 tbsps olive oil

1. Blend the first 7 ingredients together.
2. Add the oil and blend well.
3. Serve in a gravy boat alongside grilled filet mignon, shish kebabs or hamburgers.

Note: The sauce will keep separating, so keep stirring it as it is served.

* * * * * * * *

VINAIGRETTE SAUCE

The following is an ideal dipping sauce for artichokes. Although typically French, it is commonly used in European Moroccan households.

Makes 1½ cups

3–4 tbsps Dijon or Dusseldorf mustard

¾ cup oil

Coarse salt to taste

Fresh black pepper to taste

2 tbsps wine vinegar, or to taste

1. Put the mustard in a small mixing bowl. Gradually beat in the oil, adding it drop by drop, so that the oil becomes incorporated into the mustard and the mixture becomes thick and glossy. If the oil is added too quickly, it may cause the vinaigrette to separate, which is undesirable.
2. Add the salt and pepper to taste.
3. Gradually stir in the wine vinegar to taste.

VINAIGRETTE SALAD DRESSING

Herewith another French salad dressing. This one is exceptionally tasty tossed with grated carrots. Salad dressing is one instance in which Mme. Elmaleh specified the use of olive oil. She preferred it for green salads, rather than peanut oil, which she favored for cooking.

Makes enough for 1 salad

1 tbsp Dijon mustard
2 tbsps vinegar
1 tsp salt
Fresh black pepper to taste
4 tbsps olive oil

1. Blend the first 4 ingredients together well.
2. Add the oil and blend again.

* * * * * * * * *

CAPER MAYONNAISE FOR FRIED FISH

Makes ½ cup

3 tbsp mayonnaise
1 tsp horseradish
1 tsp lemon juice
½ tsp sugar
1 tbsp capers, chopped
1 tbsp parsley, minced or 1 tbsp fresh dill, minced
1 tbsp onion, grated
Salt to taste

1. Blend the above ingredients and chill until serving time.

PRESERVES

SPICED PEAR COMPOTE
(Lingas)

These pears magically turn a bright rosy pink when cooked. It is customary to serve the compote alongside or just after a meat course, however they also make a fine dessert.

1 dozen (or more, if desired) very firm pears, such as Bartlett, Bosc, Anjou or Seckel, peeled, cored and sliced into thick wedges

2 tart firm apples, such as Granny Smith or Greening (optional), peeled, cored and sliced into thick wedges

1 rind of a lemon, slivered into ¼" strips

3–4 whole cloves

1½ cups sugar

Water to cover

Mason jars, sterilized, with close-fitting lids

1. Place all of the ingredients into a wide, heavy saucepan.
2. Bring all to a boil and allow to cook down over a slow fire, uncovered, stirring occasionally, until the compote thickens and turns deep pink in color. Be careful; the compote will caramelize and turn brownish if it has cooked too long.
3. Put pears into the jars and pour the juice over them just to cover.
4. After each jar has been opened, store the remainder of the compote in the refrigerator.

* * * * * * * *

GLACÉED GRAPEFRUIT
(Mazhoun)

These are glistening chunks of tangy, caramelized grapefruit. Also served alongside a meat course, their unique pungency clears the palate at the end of a meal.

SERVES 12–20

3 grapefruit
1 tbsp coarse salt
Cold water to cover
3 cups sugar
Mason jars, sterilized, with close-fitting lids

1. Thinly zest the outer yellow skin from the grapefruit, leaving the white pulp intact. (Failure to remove this thin yellow outer layer will cause the end product to taste bitter.)

2. Place the grapefruit in a pot with the cold water to cover and the salt. Allow them to stand for 30 minutes. This will remove some of the bitterness from the pulp.

3. Bring this water to a boil and then discard it. Cover the grapefruit again with fresh water this time and repeat this process. Repeat this process once more, the third time boiling the fruits a little longer so that the membranes become tender.

4. Rinse the grapefruit in cold water. Place each on a board and slice each one into six wedges. Try to remove the membranes and the seeds very gently so as not to shred the pulp.

5. Put the sugar in the pot with water just to cover it. Bring it to a boil.

6. Meanwhile, take two pieces of grapefruit at a time and press them together 'pulp to pulp' to squeeze out all of their liquid. Continue this process for all of the grapefruit.

7. When the sugar has come to a boil, place the grapefruit wedges into the syrup, skin side down.

8. Keep turning the pieces over a low fire until they become very golden and thickly caramelized.

9. Store the *mazhoun* in the sterilized jars in a cool place. After opening a jar, store the remainder of the conserve in the refrigerator. These keep forever.

GLACÉED ORANGES
(Orange Mazhoun)

This version is slightly sweeter, but no less delicious. Follow the same recipe as for the grapefruit, except use six navel oranges instead of three grapefruit. If the syrup needs additional thickening, add extra sugar while the fruits are cooking.

* * * * * * * * *

CHOCOLATE-COVERED GLACÉED FRUITS

1/2 cup Glacéed Grapefruit (*Mazhoun*)
1/2 cup Glacéed Orange (*Mazhoun*)
1/2 cup crystallized candied ginger
5 oz (150 g) semi-sweet chocolate morsels (or other chocolate of choice)

1. Sliver the grapefruit, orange and ginger pieces into thin translucent strips, about $1\frac{1}{2}$–2 inches long and about $\frac{1}{8}$–$\frac{1}{4}$ inches wide.
2. Melt the chocolate in the top of a double boiler until it is smooth and creamy.
3. One by one, dip the candied fruit strips about halfway into the melted chocolate, allowing about half of the fruit to still show.
4. On a wide tray, place each strip onto a foil or waxed paper sheet to cool, making sure that each strip stays separate.
5. If time is a concern, store the tray of fruit in the refrigerator to cool down more quickly.
6. Arrange them on a serving platter in a snowflake pattern, or add them to a platter of the stuffed date 'petit-fours'. They look most appealing when sticking up vertically, like little spikes, sandwiched in and among the stuffed dates or other dried fruit.

CANDIED KUMQUATS

1 quart kumquats, leaves and stems removed
1 cup sugar
Water to cover

1. In a wide, heavy saucepan place the sugar with enough water just to cover it.

2. Bring the mixture to a boil until it is syrupy, then add the kumquats. Let the kumquats simmer over a slow fire, covered, until they are thickly glazed. Stir them occasionally as they cook, to make sure they become glazed evenly.

3. When they are just tender, remove them from the stove. Let the kumquats cool to room temperature, then store them in the refrigerator.

QUINCE COMPOTE AND JELLY
(Makhouda)

In addition to being a delectable accompaniment to any meal, the quince's pink liquid was also claimed by my grandmother to be a remedy for stomach ulcers. Well, it certainly palliates the taste buds.

SERVES 12

6 quince, washed and sliced into six wedges each, seeds removed and set aside

Water to cover

2 cups sugar

Mason jars, sterilized, with tight-fitting lids

1. Place all ingredients in a wide, heavy saucepan. Bring all to a boil, then simmer, uncovered, until the fruit is tender and the flesh is pink. The simmering takes about 30 minutes. The quince itself is now ready to be served warm or else to be chilled in the refrigerator.

2. To make jelly from the quince liquid, wrap the quince seeds in a small piece of cheesecloth and fasten it with toothpicks. Add this to the liquid and continue cooking along with the fruit. These seeds will help gel the liquid.

3. When the liquid has gelled, pour the jelly into the mason jars. Let cool slightly, then seal. For an extra treat, however, proceed to the following recipe.

quince

QUINCE CANDIES

Quince jelly from previous recipe, fruit removed
1 cup flaked coconut

1. Continue to boil down the jelly from the previous recipe. It will thicken even further.
2. When the consistency becomes hard enough, break off little hunks of it and roll them in the coconut. Continue this process for all of the jelly.
3. Arrange the candies on a platter. Cover with plastic wrap or waxed paper and refrigerate until serving time.

* * * * * * * * *

HEAVENLY FRUIT AND NUT CONSERVE

This absolutely heady concoction can be used either as a spread or as a mouth-watering pie filling, as in my grandmother's 'Linzer Torte à la Mogadorienne' (see recipe).

1 lb (450 g) concord grapes, well-washed
3 oranges, seeded and sliced into thin wedges
2 wedges orange mazhoun (see recipe)
3–4 apples, peeled, cored, seeded and chopped
6 cups sugar
½ tsp cinnamon
1 cup walnut meats, chopped coarsely
Mason jars, sterilized, with tight-fitting lids

1. Bring the grapes to a boil in a pot with water to cover. Stir the pot to loosen the skins and the seeds from the pulp. Boil the pulp and force it through a strainer to remove the seeds.
2. Put the skins through a food chopper along with the apple and the orange pieces.
3. Put all the fruit back into the pot with the six cups of sugar and the cinnamon.
4. Cook the mixture over a slow fire, uncovered, until it has thickened to taste. Then stir in the nut meats.
5. Store in the mason jars. Refrigerate the jars after opening them.

DESSERTS

The most typical after-dinner treat for Moroccans is a simple basket of their native fruits. My mother was raised with the French expression *'le meilleur confiseur, c'est le Bon Dieu'* — 'the best dessert-maker is God Himself'. One taste of a delicate clementine or succulent Medjhoul date is enough to prove that it is true. Herewith some of Morocco's natural delights:

MOROCCAN FRUIT BASKET

Dates, preferably the large sweet Medjhoul variety

Bananas, small but very sweet (indigenous to the Souss region)

Oranges, known as 'the pride of Marrakesh'

Tangerines

Mandarines, smaller than tangerines and very juicy

Clementines, smaller still, with paper-thin skin and no seeds

Fresh or Dried figs

Barbary figs — cactus berries, which must be 'de-prickled' before serving. Greenish to reddish on the outside, they are lusciously pink and juicy inside.

Sweet lemons — although scarce, these can sometimes be found in markets in Southern Morocco. They look exactly like normal lemons, except that they have a sweet and rather mellow flavor.

The Moroccans, like many Europeans, are accustomed to having their main meal at midday followed by a light meal later in the evening at, say, seven or eight o'clock. To punctuate the long hours between lunch and supper, they look forward to their daily teatime at four or five o'clock. The Moslem people are particularly fond of their mint tea, liberally sweetened, which provides them with a lift throughout the day. (Consumption of alcohol, it must be remembered, is not permitted in Islam.)

In Mogador, the fashionable ladies of the town adopted, or rather seized upon, the British custom of serving tea with elaborate pastries for social get-togethers. It became a form of social one-upmanship; the gossip would travel so fast in the small town that by evening everyone knew, for example, that Madam So-and-so had served fourteen different pastries for tea that afternoon.

The recipes in this section would most ordinarily accompany a Moroccan afternoon tea, whereas we westerners might prefer to serve them as desserts after dinner.

CRISP HONEY SWIRLS
(Chebbakia)

These crunchy serpentine spirals fairly oozing with honey are a special delight for children.

1 cake of yeast, dissolved in ½ cup hot (110°F) water

2–3 cups flour, approximately

¼ tsp salt

Water

2 eggs, lightly beaten

2 teaspoons <u>saffron water</u> (see recipe)

2 cups matzo meal or cracker meal

½ tsp salt

4 egg yolks, lightly beaten

4 egg whites, at room temperature

Oil for deep frying

1 ½ cups honey

Cinnamon

1. In a large bowl, blend the yeast solution, the flour, the two beaten eggs and the ¼ teaspoonful of salt. Stir it together to form a dough. Keep adding lukewarm water and stirring until it spoons up loosely like a pancake batter.

2. Cover the batter with a damp towel and allow it to rise for 8 hours or overnight.

3. After the batter has risen for the allotted time, stir in the saffron water to color the dough yellow, the matzo meal, the ½ teaspoonful of salt, the egg yolks, and enough lukewarm water to loosen up the batter again.

4. In a separate bowl, beat the egg whites until they are stiff but not dry. Fold them gently into the batter.

5. Heat a ½-inch depth of oil in a wide skillet (pan or frying-pan).

6. Working quickly, pour the batter into the skillet in a concentric circular pattern, starting in the center and spiralling outward toward the edges of the skillet. Fry it until it is golden. Then, using a wide spatula, remove the fried batter spiral, drain it slightly over the skillet, and remove it to paper toweling to drain further.

7. Continue to repeat the above process until all of the batter is used up.

8. While the *chebbakia* are still warm, heat the honey in another wide skillet, and dip each pastry into it briefly. Then remove them to a wide serving platter and sprinkle them all over with cinnamon.

ORANGE SHERBET CUPS À LA MAMOUNIA

These ornamental little *coupes glacées* were adapted from those served at the luxurious Mamounia Hotel in Marrakesh. My grandmother attended many New Year's celebrations or *Réveillons* there. After a sumptuous banquet, these temptingly frosted fruits would refresh even the most jaded taste buds.

SERVES 6

6 thick-skinned, preferably navel, oranges
2 pints orange or lemon sherbet
6 sprigs of fresh mint

1. Slice the tops from the oranges, about ¼ of the way down. Slice a thin layer from the bottom of each orange so that they will stand evenly.
2. With a grapefruit knife or other serrated knife, carefully cut out all the fruit inside. Reserve the fruit for a fruit salad or other use.
3. Fill each orange cup with a scoop of sherbet, rounding it smoothly on top.
4. These may be frozen at this point and served at a later time. When serving, press a sprig of fresh mint into each orange cup to decorate.

MOUSSE AU CHOCOLAT

Confirmed chocoholics such as the entire Elmaleh clan prefer their chocolate as 'undiluted' as possible. Therefore, my mother, Helene Elmaleh Craig (a terrific cook in her own right), varied this classic French recipe to exclude the heavy cream. This simple, yet sinful, dessert remains a must at all our family gatherings.

SERVES 6

6 eggs, separated, at room temperature

12 oz (350 g) semi-sweet chocolate, broken into small pieces

1 tbsp sweet butter (optional)

¼ cup rum, Kahlua, or Grand Marnier liqueur (optional)

1–2 tsps instant coffee powder

Candied violets, optional

1. Melt the chocolate in the top of a double-boiler over boiling water. If it needs softening, add a little butter. Stir the mixture with a wooden spoon to break up any lumps.

2. In the meantime, beat the yolks in a large mixing bowl until they are light and frothy. Stir this mixture into the chocolate mixture, working quickly so that the cool eggs do not stiffen the chocolate.

3. In a separate bowl, with cleaned-off beater blades, beat the egg whites into stiff peaks.

4. Add the liquor and the coffee powder to the chocolate mixture and blend well.

5. Using a large spoon or spatula, gently fold the egg whites into the chocolate mixture. Be careful not to stir too quickly; this can cause the fragile egg whites to 'deflate'.

6. When the mousse is uniformly folded together, pour it into a decorative serving bowl or into individual dessert cups (Champagne glasses look especially elegant).

7. Garnish the dessert with candied violets as desired. Cover the bowl(s) with plastic wrap to prevent a hard skin from forming on top, and chill the dessert for at least 2 to 3 hours before serving. Leftovers keep beautifully in the refrigerator for a week or more.

Note: This is one of the rare times that Grandma Elmaleh permitted alcohol in a recipe.

LEMON WALNUT MERINGUE TORTE

Containing no butter or cream, this majestic dessert makes a spectacular finish to even the strictest kosher feast. Be sure to prepare the meringues on a dry day.

SERVES 8–10

9 eggs, separated
1 pinch salt
3½ cups sugar
1 tsp cream of tartar
Grated rind of 2 lemons
Juice of 2 lemons
1 packet natural gelatine, dissolved in 1 tbsp hot (110°F) water
1 cup chopped walnuts
Cinnamon

1. Preheat oven to 200°F.
2. In a large bowl, beat the nine egg whites with a pinch of salt. Add the cream of tartar. Gradually beat in 2½ cups of sugar. Keep beating until the peaks are very stiff and glossy.
3. Grease two baking sheets with a little margarine or oil. (The disposable type of baking sheets are perfect for this because they can easily be peeled away from the baked meringue layers.) Trace three 10-inch circles onto waxed paper. Cut them out, grease them on both sides and place them on the baking sheets.
4. Spread the meringue out onto the circles, distributing it evenly, and smoothing the meringue layers with a spatula to make them uniform in thickness all around. Build a slightly raised rim around the edges of two of the layers; this will help later on to contain the filling.
5. Bake them at 200°F until the layers become stiff but not too hard, from 1 to 2 hours. If they start to brown too quickly, turn the oven off and let them stand until they are crunchy.
6. Meanwhile, in the top of a double boiler with the water boiling below, beat the 9 egg yolks with 1 cup of sugar, using a hand mixer over the stove.

7. Add the lemon juice and rind and the gelatine. Beat until very thick and light. It will rise to the top of the pot.

8. Cool and refrigerate the egg mixture.

9. Remove the meringue layers from the oven when they are crispy and still light-colored. Allow the layers to cool to room temperature, then carefully peel off the waxed paper from underneath.

10. Spread the cooled egg mixture onto the two cooled meringue layers with the built-up rims. Sprinkle the walnuts evenly over this custard.

11. Place one of these layers on top of the other on a serving platter, and place the third layer on top of those.

12. Sprinkle cinnamon on top to decorate. Refrigerate until serving time. This torte may even be placed in the freezer for 1 hour or so to prevent the custard from becoming too runny. When serving, slice the torte very carefully using a serrated knife.

GRANDMA'S ENGLISH 'PIE'

Folks from Mogador actually call this confection a 'pie', although in fact it is a version of England's beloved 'trifle'. It is no doubt a legacy from the days when the British inhabited the North African seaport.

SERVES 10-12

5 eggs, separated
2 cups sugar
Juice of 2 lemons
Rind of 2 lemons
½ jar raspberry jam
2 loaves of spongecake, sliced into ¼" slices
1 qt jar mixed fruit compote, liquid reserved
¼ cup rum or whiskey, optional, or orange-blossom water

1. Preheat the oven to 250°F.
2. In the top of a double boiler over boiling water, use a hand mixer to beat the 5 egg yolks with ¾ cup of the sugar, the lemon juice and the rind. When it is very thick and it rises to the top of the pot, remove the custard from the heat.
3. On the bottom of an ovenproof oval serving platter, about 12 inches long and at least ¾ inch deep, make a layer of the spongecake slices. Mix the reserved fruit juice with the ¼ cup of liquor, and drizzle some of it over the spongecake layer.
4. Spread a thin layer of raspberry jam on the spongecake. Then make an even layer of the fruit. Over this, spread a layer of custard. Keep layering in this fashion until all the spongecake, juice, fruit and custard are used up.
5. Beat the egg whites with 1½ cups of sugar. Beat until the peaks become stiff but not dry. Mound the meringue on top of the trifle layers, shaping it decoratively with a spoon. Sprinkle the top with cinnamon.
6. Place the platter in the oven at 250°F for 30 minutes, or until the meringue forms a crust on top. Allow the 'pie' to come to room temperature before serving.

HEAVENLY FRUIT PIE WITH WALNUTS
(Tortas 'Linzer torte' à la Mogadorienne)

SERVES 8

2 cups <u>Heavenly Fruit and Nut Conserve</u> (see recipe)
1 egg, lightly beaten
1 tbsp sugar
1 tsp baking powder
1 pinch salt
Flour enough to bind into a dough
10–12 walnut halves

1. Preheat the oven to 350°F.
2. In a large bowl, mix together the sugar, baking powder and salt.
3. Add 1 cup of flour and cut in the butter with a fork.
4. Add the egg and blend well. Add more flour, enough to make a firm ball of dough.
5. Roll the dough out onto a floured surface and make a circle of about 1/8-inch thickness. Fit it into a flat tart pan. Reserve the extra dough.
6. Fill the pastry with the jam, spreading it evenly.
7. Use any extra dough to roll out and slice into flat strips. Criss-cross these strips over the top of the pie to decorate.
8. Intersperse the criss-crosses with the walnut halves until each empty space is filled.
9. Bake the pie at 350°F for 30 minutes.

CHESTNUT CAKE

Subtle and moist with a distinctive brown-sugary crust, this is truly a connoisseur's cake.

SERVES 10-12

1 quart of chestnuts
1 cup oil
6 cups water
6–7 eggs, separated
1 cup sugar
1 tsp cinnamon
¾ cup dark brown sugar, packed firm

1. With a sharp, pointed knife, gash the skin on the flat side of each chestnut, making an 'X' mark. In a large skillet (pan or frying pan), heat the oil. Add the chestnuts to the hot oil and, shaking the pan constantly, toast them over a high heat for about 7 minutes. Drain them and let them cool enough to be handled. Remove the shells and the inner skins.

2. Bring the chestnuts to a boil in a saucepan with the six cups of water. Boil them until they are tender, and then drain. Grind the chestnuts in a grinder.

3. Preheat the oven to 350°F.

4. Beat the egg whites into peaks that are stiff but not dry.

5. In a separate bowl, beat together the yolks, the cup of sugar and the cinnamon until light and frothy.

6. Add the ground chestnuts to the yolk mixture and beat well.

7. Gently fold the egg whites into the yolk mixture.

8. Grease a spring-form pan and put an even layer of the brown sugar over the bottom.

9. Gently pour the batter over the top. Tap the pan on the sides to make sure that the batter is level.

10. Bake the cake at 350°F for about 45 minutes, or until it springs back when touched in the center.

ALMOND CAKE

4 cups blanched almonds
Rind of 1½ lemons
5 eggs, separated
1 cup sugar

1. Preheat the oven to 350°F.
2. Grind the almonds in a grinder together with the lemon peels.
3. Beat the egg whites until the peaks are stiff but not dry.
4. In a separate bowl, beat the yolks with the sugar until light and fluffy. Add the ground almond mixture and blend well.
5. Gently fold the egg whites into the yolk mixture.
6. Pour this batter into a greased and floured bundt or spring-form pan.
7. Bake the cake at 350°F for 35 to 40 minutes, or until it springs back when touched in the center.

MERINGUES

These gossamer confections should be crispy on the outside and creamy in the center. They are most successful when prepared on a dry day.

MAKES 20

4 egg whites
1 cup sugar
Cinnamon

1. Preheat the oven to 200°F.
2. Beat the egg whites until foamy. Add the sugar little by little so that it dissolves properly, and keep beating until the white peaks are satiny.
3. Spoon the meringues into 3-inch by 2-inch oval shapes onto ungreased foil baking sheets.
4. Place them in the oven. After 30 minutes, tap the top of one of them to see if they have hardened. Then close the oven, shut off the heat and leave them inside for another 2 hours.
5. Let them cool to room temperature, gently remove them from the baking sheet, and serve. They should be stored in an airtight container in a cool, dry place.

CARAWAY TEA BISCUITS

MAKES ABOUT 3 DOZEN (DEPENDING ON SIZE)

4 eggs
½ cup sugar
½ cup oil
1tsp caraway seeds
2 tbsps baking powder
Flour enough to make a stiff dough
Sugar

1. Preheat the oven to 250°F.
2. Blend all of the ingredients and knead the dough very well until it is smooth and elastic.
3. On a smooth floured surface, roll the dough out to a 3/16-inch thickness.
4. Cut out the cookies either with a cookie cutter or with the rim of a glass. Continue re-rolling and cutting until all of the dough is used up.
5. Dip the top side of each cookie into a saucer of sugar. Place the cookies on greased cookie sheets.
6. Bake at 250°F for 30 minutes.
7. Store the cookies in an air-tight container in a cool, dry place.

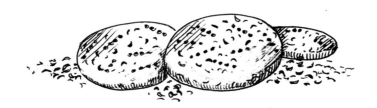

CINNAMON MACAROONS

3 cups toasted almonds
1 tsp orange flower water
¾ cup sugar
3 egg whites
½ tsp vanilla
2 tsps cinnamon
1 lemon rind or 1 orange rind, grated
1 cup confectioners' (icing) sugar

1. Preheat the oven to 300°F.
2. Grind the almonds and the orange flower water together to make a paste. Add more orange flower water if necessary.
3. Blend all the ingredients except the confectioners' sugar. Knead the dough very well for a few minutes.
4. Let the dough rest for 1–2 hours at room temperature. Place a damp cloth or towel over the bowl to keep the dough from drying up.
5. Coat both hands with a little oil and roll the dough into 1-inch balls.
6. Roll each ball in the confectioners' sugar.
7. Place them on ungreased cookie sheets and bake them at 300°F for 30 minutes, or until slightly golden at the edge.
8. When cooled, store the macaroons in an airtight container.

SESAME COOKIES
(Helwah d'Zinslan)

Some Arab cultures believe that sesame seeds are an aphrodisiac, and after all, Morocco is a country in which witch doctors, with their love potions and other bizarre herbal and animal remedies, have a place side by side in the souks with the westernized pharmacies.

These may or may not improve one's love life, but they are nonetheless habit-forming.

MAKES ABOUT 30

2 cups sugar
½ cup honey
6 cups toasted sesame seeds
1 cup walnuts, chopped

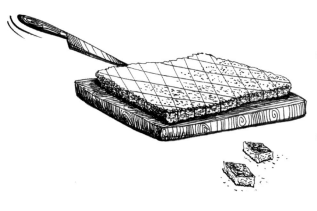

1. In a wide, heavy saucepan, melt the sugar. Over a slow fire, melt it into a golden brown caramel. Take care not to let it burn.
2. Add the honey and blend it in.
3. When the mixture begins to foam up, turn down the fire and begin stirring in the sesame seeds and the walnuts. Do this gradually to make sure that all the seeds and nuts get coated with the caramel.
4. Working quickly, pour the mixture out onto a wet cutting board. With a rolling pin, roll the mixture out into a ½-inch thickness.
5. Let the mixture cool for a minute. With a sharp, pointed knife, slice the dough diagonally into strips, about 1½ inches wide. Then, following the opposite diagonal, cut those strips into diamond shapes.
6. Place the diamond shaped cookies onto one or two serving platters. Cover tightly with plastic wrap or waxed paper and store at room temperature. They are supposed to be crisp, but they may become slightly elastic and sticky.
   If necessary, layer them between sheets of waxed paper to keep the pieces separate.

HONEY CLUSTERS
(Helwah d'Zinslan)

My grandmother traditionally served these treats, along with many others, on Yom Kippur to break the fast after sundown. She always made that holiest of Jewish holidays into the 'dessert-first' day, because the family would fast all day long and the children particularly looked forward to seeing Grandpa return from temple in the evening so we could dig into all the sugary goodies. These may or may not improve one's love life, but they are nonetheless habit-forming.

Eastern European Jews make a very similar confection known as taiglach

4 eggs, lightly beaten
1 tsp baking powder
Enough flour to knead into a 5" ball
Deep oil for frying
2 cups sugar
2 tbsp honey

1. Mix the eggs and the baking powder together. Add the flour and knead it very well into a ball about 5 inches in diameter. Divide this ball into three equal parts.
2. Roll each part out onto a floured surface until it is uniformly ¼-inch thick. With a sharp pointed knife, cut the flattened dough into strips ½-inch wide. Then cut those strips cross-wise to make squares.
3. Heat the oil in a wide skillet, pan or frying pan. When it is hot enough, drop a handful of the dough pieces into the pan. Turn them until they are fried golden on all sides. Remove them and let them drain on paper toweling. Continue frying the remainder of the dough pieces in this manner.
4. In a wide, heavy saucepan, cook the sugar over a slow fire until it is golden brown and caramelized. Lower the fire and stir in the honey.

5. Stir the drained dough balls into the thickening syrup, coating them thoroughly. When the syrup is thick and threadlike, remove clusters with a large soup spoon and place them onto a moistened cutting board. Roll them or flatten them out to a 1-inch thickness. Let them cool to room temperature. With a sharp knife cut them into two-inch squares or diamond shapes.

6. Store the honey clusters airtight at room temperature. If necessary, layer them with waxed paper to keep the pieces separate.

* * * * * * * *

NOUGATINES
(Helwah d'Grgah)

1½ cups sugar

½ cup honey

4 cups walnuts and/or almonds (toast them in the oven at 250°F for 30 minutes if necessary to make them crunchy)

1. Melt down the sugar in a heavy saucepan over a slow fire. When it becomes golden brown, stir in the honey.

2. Quickly stir in the nuts so that they are thoroughly coated.

3. Spread the nut mixture out onto a wet cutting board. Drop the nuts by teaspoonfuls onto a serving platter, or into individual paper candy cups.

4. Let them cool to room temperature to harden. Store the nougatines in an airtight container.

CINNAMON PASTRY CURLS
(Faduelos)

MAKES 15 PIECES

2–3 eggs, slightly beaten
1 tbsp water
Pinch of salt
1 tsp baking soda
Enough flour to make a stiff dough ball 3½ inches in diameter (1½ cups or more)
Oil for deep-frying
2 cups sugar
¼ cup water
Cinnamon

1. Mix together the eggs, water, salt and baking soda. Add enough flour to shape the mixture into a stiff ball of dough about 3½ inches in diameter.

2. Divide the dough into three equal parts. Roll each part, one at a time, onto a floured board. Roll each piece of dough out to a thickness of about 1/16 of an inch. With a pastry wheel, cut the dough lengthwise into strips about 2 inches wide and about 16 to 18 inches long.

3. Heat the oil for deep frying. Fasten the end of one strip of dough through the tines of a long fork, and dip it into the hot oil. Keep twirling the dough around the fork as it fries; it will harden into a spiral shape. When it turns golden and crisp all over, remove the pastry to paper toweling to drain. Continue the same procedure for all of the remaining dough strips. Let them drain until they become very dry.

4. Meanwhile, dissolve the 2 cups of sugar in the ¼ cup of water in a heavy saucepan over a slow fire. Bring the mixture to a boil until it becomes threadlike, but still clear in color. If necessary, put an asbestos pad over the flame to keep the sugar from overcooking and becoming caramelized.

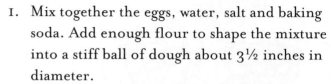

5. Dip each pastry curl into the sugar syrup. Shake it over the pan to drain off any excess. Remove the *faduelos* to a large serving platter and sprinkle them liberally with cinnamon. Let them cool to room temperature and serve. Store them at room temperature in airtight containers.

* * * * * * * * *

GAZELLE HORN COOKIES
(Kab El Ghzal)

1 cup almonds, blanched
½ cup sugar
1 egg
¼ tsp salt
Flour enough to make a stiff dough
Confectioners' (icing) sugar

1. Grind the almonds in a grinder twice.
2. In a small heavy saucepan, add the ground almonds and the sugar and cook them together over a slow fire until the sugar has dissolved in the almond mixture. Set aside to cool.
3. In a mixing bowl, blend together the egg, salt and enough flour to make a firm ball of dough.
4. Roll the dough out onto a floured surface until it is a uniform 1/16-inch thickness. Using a tiny saucer or other circular object, trace circles in the dough about 3-3½ inches in diameter with a pie-crust trimmer.
5. Repeat the above process until all of the dough is used up.
6. Preheat the oven to 350°F.
7. Place a small strip of the almond mixture on half of a pastry circle, folding the other half over it like an envelope. Crimp the edges together with the pastry

edger or the tines of a fork or else seal them by moistening them with a little water.

8. Repeat this process to use up all of the dough and the filling.
9. Place the cookies on greased baking sheets.
10. Bake at 350°F for about 15 minutes or until crisp but not browned. While they are still warm, roll them in the confectioners' sugar. Store the cookies airtight in a cool, dry place.

* * * * * * * * *

GLACÉED FRUITS

Grandma learned to make these crystalline treasures from her lifelong friend Mme. Rosita Senouf. They are beautiful to behold, but even better are their crunchy-juicy texture and succulent fruit flavors.

MAKES 40–50 PIECES

40 lumps of sugar
Water to cover
1 tbsp vinegar
Assorted pieces of fruit: (40–50 pieces)
   Tangerine sections
   Grapes
   <u>Prunes (pitted) stuffed</u>, if desired (see recipe)
   <u>Dates (pitted) stuffed</u>, if desired (see recipe)

1. In a heavy saucepan, dissolve the sugar in the water to cover. Let it cook over a very slow fire, stirring in the vinegar, until it becomes threadlike when poured from a spoon. Do not allow it to color or caramelize.
2. While the sugar mixture is warm, dip the pieces of fruit in one at a time, coating each piece thoroughly.
3. After dipping, place each piece of the fruit onto a sheet of waxed paper, and allow them to harden crystal clear. Serve them when they get to room temperature. They are fragile and do not keep for a long time, but any leftovers should be stored in an airtight container.

TRADITIONAL STUFFED DATES AND PRUNES

If there is a favorite confection among all Moroccans, this is probably the one. Ladies take pride in creating their own original designs with the almond paste, and they actually refer to them as 'petit fours'. These daintily crafted candies make a colorful display; trays of them are often presented as house gifts.

MAKES ABOUT 40 PIECES

2 cups almonds
Rind of ½ lemon
1 cup sugar
Green and red food coloring
Walnut halves
20 prunes, pitted
20 dates, pitted
Granulated sugar

1. To blanch the almonds, pour boiling water on them and cover them for about 5 minutes, then peel off the skins.
2. Rinse them in cold water and dry them well.
3. Grind them in a grinder with the lemon rind. Add the sugar to this mixture and grind it again. Divide the almond paste into 3 portions. Add a tiny drop of green food coloring to one portion, a tiny drop of red to the second portion, and leave the third portion natural, if desired. Knead the fillings well to make even pastel colors.
4. Roll the fillings into tiny oblong pieces that fit into the cavities of the fruits. Press walnut halves on top of the fillings to decorate. Press the fruits back into shape.
5. Either glaze the dates and prunes as in the Glacéed Fruits recipe, or roll each piece in granulated sugar. Serve at room temperature and refrigerate any leftovers.

QUICK STUFFED DATES AND PRUNES

Here is a modern shortcut:

1 can (8oz; 225 g) almond paste
¼ cup light corn syrup
1 cup confectioners' (icing) sugar
Red, green and yellow food coloring
20 dates, pitted
20 prunes, pitted
Walnut halves
Granulated sugar

1. Knead the almond paste, syrup and confectioners' (icing) sugar into a paste. Separate the filling into three equal portions and add one tiny drop of food coloring into each. Knead them well to make even pastel colors.
2. Shape the fillings into small oblongs that fit into the cavities of the fruits. Insert them into the prunes and dates, and top each with a walnut half, if desired.
3. Roll them in the granulated sugar and store them airtight in a cool place or in the refrigerator.

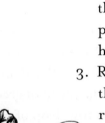

❋ ❋ ❋ ❋ ❋ ❋ ❋ ❋ ❋

DATES STUFFED WITH WALNUTS

These may be the original 'healthfood' candies. They are so simple to make yet so rich-tasting.

MAKES 20

20 dates, preferably the Medjhoul variety, pitted
20 walnut halves
Granulated sugar, optional

1. Stuff a walnut half into each date cavity.
2. Either roll them in the granulated sugar or serve them just plain. Store the remainder in the refrigerator.

MINT TEA
(Té Na'nah)

No Moroccan meal is complete without its tea ceremony. In some native households, it is brewed with 'shiba' or 'old man's beard', an herb which supposedly tastes like absinthe. Mint tea is traditionally poured from a curvaceously shaped pewter or silver teapot into small intricately designed tea-glasses, and served on a shimmering hand-carved brass tray. A proper tea service is every bit as important to the Moroccans as it is to the English or the Japanese people.

MAKES 3–4 CUPS

Boiling water

1½ tbsps green tea

3–4 sprigs of fresh mint

1–1/3 cups sugar cubes (Note: those preferring it less sweet should omit some of the sugar to taste)

1. Rinse out the teapot with hot water.
2. Put the tea leaves in a strainer and put them in the teapot. Pour ½ a cup of boiling water into the pot, swirl it around quickly and empty out the water. (This removes any initial bitterness from the tea leaves.)
3. Put the mint leaves and stalks into the pot with the sugar to taste. Fill the pot with the boiling water and allow the tea to steep for 5 to 8 minutes, depending on the potency desired.
4. Stir and add sugar to taste. Serve.

mint
(nanah)

CINNAMON-SUGAR AMBROSIA TOPPING FOR COFFEE
(L'Beid Emderbah)

It all started as our family's way to break the day-long fast of Yom Kippur, but now, never a holiday goes by without this pièce de résistance. Affectionately known by the family as 'coffee glop', this is actually a sugary whipped egg custard that we ladle and swirl into our hot, black coffee after dinner. We believe it is somehow related to Italian 'zabaglione'. We Elmalehs like it sweet and by the pailful.

1 egg yolk per serving (use leftover whites for meringues or another purpose)

Sugar

Cinnamon

1. Beat the egg yolks very, very well until they are very light-colored and frothy.
2. Begin adding the sugar, teaspoon by teaspoon (figure about 2 teaspoonfuls of sugar per yolk) and beat it in very well until the sugar granules dissolve. The mixture should be thick and light.
3. Add 1 to 2 teaspoonfuls of cinnamon (or to taste) and blend very well.
4. Correct for sweetness and add extra sugar, if desired.
5. Pour the mixture into a decorative glass serving bowl and sprinkle cinnamon on top to decorate.
6. Serve at room temperature. Ladle tablespoonfuls onto hot cups of coffee, and let each person swirl it in or spoon it up as desired.

HERBAL REMEDIES

OLIVE OIL REMEDY FOR BRONCHITIS

Living in a wet and windy seaport town, the Elmaleh children grew up with their share of coughs and colds. Actually, the infant mortality rate was quite high, due to pleurisy and pneumonia. However unfondly, they remember having to take this:

1 raw egg
½ cup boiling water
1 tsp olive oil
Pinch of salt

1. First thing in the morning, pour boiling water on the raw egg in a glass.
2. Add the olive oil, the salt, and stir well.
3. Drink it (quickly). Repeat this process first thing in the morning for three days in a row.
   This relieves bad coughs and congested lungs.

* * * * * * * *

My grandmother's grandmother, Mme. Myriam 'Ramo' Abenaim, was an herbalist of great renown in the Mogador region, in a time and place where modern physicians and 'wonder drugs' were almost non-existent. In the late 1800s, long before the advent of penicillin, this resourceful woman stored crocks of rancid butter, which she allowed to become green with mold. From this mold she made an ointment, which she applied to her patients with skin inflammations, thereby curing their various rashes, abscesses, and even venereal disease. Little did anyone know that this was the precursor of penicillin.

Mme. Abenaim also cultivated a special variety of crocus from which she extracted a milky sap. When she applied this sap to the eyes of cataract patients, the cataracts miraculously separated themselves from the surface of the eye. She then slid them off easily with a wooden wand: no surgery was necessary.

To cure typhus fever she used live snails collected from the rocky seashore. Much as western doctors employed leeches, she applied the snails to the affected areas of the victim's body to 'absorb' the high temperatures of the fever.

Kidney ailments were successfully treated with quantities of brewed corn silk infusions; acute diarrhea was cured with powdered pomegranate skin, and headache sufferers were relieved by wearing vinegar-soaked bandannas around their foreheads.

Did these remedies survive because our ancestors survived, or vice versa? Herewith a few of the 'cures' which have been used successfully and passed down through the generations.

※ ※ ※ ※ ※ ※ ※ ※

ONION-THYME REMEDY FOR STOMACH AILMENTS
(Besla o Zaater)

With this brewed concoction, Grandma cured her friends and family members of their bouts with stomach cramps, indigestion, and even one friend's chronic colitis condition. (No promises, but it may be worth a try.)

1 tsp raw onion, grated
1 tsp dried thyme leaves
Sugar to taste, if desired
1 cup boiling water

1. Early in the morning before eating anything else, eat the 1 teaspoonful of grated onion.
2. Brew the thyme in the cup of boiling water. Let it steep a little like a tea, then add sugar to taste, if necessary. Drink it.
3. Repeat the above procedure first thing in the morning for three days straight, and the symptoms will be relieved.

ARTICHOKE REMEDY FOR LIVER AILMENTS

Grandma's own grandmother, a renowned herbalist and healer in her day, developed this cure for hepatitis symptoms. The wealthier Moroccans who suffered from rich diets of oils and chocolates often used to go to Vichy to cure their livers. They would be treated with a medicine called 'Hepascol François'. For the less privileged, there was my ancestor's acclaimed cure. If nothing else, it is a very effective diuretic.

2–3 artichokes
Water to cover

1. Boil the artichokes in a large pot with enough water to cover. Boil them, covered, for about 30 minutes.
2. Drain their cooking liquid into a jar and refrigerate it.
3. Drink a cup of the liquid once in the morning and once before bedtime for three days straight.

SOME HOMEMADE BEAUTY TREATMENTS

Grandma always prided herself on not wearing make-up; indeed, with her dark eyes and smooth skin she never needed to. However, she did glean some interesting beauty secrets from a culture in which modern cosmetics were rarely available, if at all. These natural concoctions may be enlightening to readers who are proponents of organic ingredients.

To condition the hair and soften the skin, Moroccan women have always used ghassoul, a variety of clay-based stone, which when diluted with water forms a fine, silty mud. This makes an excellent crème rinse for the hair, leaving the hair silky and shining. Ghassoul is also applied as a mud-pack for the face. When it has dried up, it must be rinsed off, thereby tightening the pores and leaving the skin very smooth.

Grandma recalled that another variety of mud-pack was made from the cowrie shells that were brought north by natives of Mauritania. Evidently, these shells were dissolved in a little lemon juice to form a white paste. This cream was similarly applied to the face as a mask to refresh the skin and tighten the pores.

To combat dryness, Arab women have always used olive oil, externally as well as internally. It lends suppleness to their olive skin, and a once-a-month overnight application of it keeps their raven-black hair looking very lustrous.

Hair (and skin) dyeing was and still is done with henna. Indeed, today many commercial hair-conditioning products contain this herb. Although its powder is greenish in color, when stirred into boiling water it gives off a reddish dye. A tablespoon of ground cloves may be added to improve the fragrance. The mud-like henna mixture is applied directly to the hair, then allowed to dry for several hours. When it is shampooed out, it leaves the hair silky and stronger, with flattering red highlights. This is especially beneficial to black or brunette hair. A caution to those with fair hair: once upon a time my grandmother's maid, Messoda, a very wrinkled woman with snow white hair and lots of gold teeth, decided to use henna. After one application, she became a rather ridiculous-looking fire-engine redhead.

In Morocco, many Arab women find it attractive to use henna to redden their palms, fingernails, knuckles, and the soles of their feet. For an added embellishment, some decorate their hands with intricate designs using a feather. These designs can last for weeks.

Bright white teeth are always a sign of beauty, even in a culture where regular dental care was in the past virtually non-existent. Before the advent of modern toothpaste, a substitute was made from sandalwood bark. After it had been burned as incense, its ashes were ground to a fine powder. This mild abrasive was used to whiten the teeth. Another natural polish was a certain tree bark, called souak, which, when chewed, not only cleaned the teeth but massaged the gums as well, making them pink and healthy-looking. People also chewed mastic, pellets of hardened tree resin which becomes more and more elastic the longer it is chewed. This may have been a forerunner of modern chewing gum, and as far as the teeth are concerned, probably more healthful.

Grandma Elmaleh also remembered how eyebrow pencil and mascara, called *harkos* was made by the Arab women. They would steam a certain variety of tree nuts (black walnuts?) called *ig* in a shallow pan with a tight-fitting lid. When sufficiently steamed, the nuts would 'sweat' off a waxy black resin which would accumulate on the inside of the lid. This substance was scraped off with a feather into a tiny container, usually a nutshell. The *harkos* was delicately applied with a feather to the eyebrows and eyelashes to blacken them.

ACKNOWLEDGEMENTS:

I would like to thank my uncle, Victor Elmaleh, whose idea it was to revive my manuscript of his mother's delicious recipes, and who supported this project through to its publication. I also want to thank the women in our family who have kept Grandma Elmaleh's cooking repertoire alive for their appreciative families. Gloria Elmaleh Fultz, Michelle Elmaleh and Terry Loewentheil, all wonderful cooks in their own right, have so kindly double-checked these recipes for me. My cousin Niko Elmaleh enlightened me on the subject of Berber history. Andree Abecassis encouraged me and supported me in this endeavour. My cousin Kerry and Uncle Earl have now perfected Grandma's *Charissa* Sauce, which is a blend of traditional Harissa with Chermoula sauce. Henceforward, this will be marketed under the name 'Charissa'. My cousin Beth currently gives lessons in Moroccan cooking. My daughters, Amanda and Antonia, have always been my willing taste-testers; I am gratified to see that they are going to carry these traditions forward to the next generation. Grandma would certainly be proud of the legacy she has left for all of us.

Last but not least, I want to thank my mother, Helene Elmaleh Craig, who is now gone but is never forgotten. She always told me, 'Lisa, no matter what you do, always do your best.'

ABOUT THE AUTHOR:

Lisa Elmaleh Craig lived in Casablanca, Morocco, as a small child, then did most of her growing up among the close-knit Elmaleh clan near her grandparents' estate on the South Shore of Long Island. She spent a great deal of time by her grandmother's side, watching her prepare exotic foods and learning about Sephardic Jewish/ French Moroccan traditions. She learned to speak French fluently but could never quite master Arabic. A graduate of Friends Academy and Middlebury College, she initially pursued a career as a freelance illustrator, then married and raised two daughters. She later earned a Masters degree in Elementary Education at Long Island University, and spent a number of years in toy design. As of this writing, she lives on Long Island's North Shore where she directs a social adult day program for elderly seniors. She is devoted to her family, her job and her dancing, and she now has three grandchildren of her own.